Oxford

Farrol Kahn

Published by
Landmark Publishing
Ashbourne Hall
Cokayne Avenue, Ashbourne
Derbyshire DE6 1EJ

W9-BIX-954

Farrol Kahn is the author of several books, including Riga and its beaches (Landmark 2000). He lives in Oxford.

ACKNOWLEDGEMENTS

The author would like to thank the following who have made the writing of this book possible: Julian Blackwell for his kind suggestions as well as the loan of precious books; Philip Blackwell; Penelope Sturgis, David Vaisey and Michael Turner at the Bodleian; Timothy Walker at the Botanic Garden; Professor Jasper Griffin at Balliol; The Very Revd John Drury, Dean and Fred Wharton at Christ Church; Professor Marilyn Butler, Rector, at Exeter; Professor Averil Cameron, Warden, Keble; Anthony Smith CBE, President, and Susan Hitch at Magdalen; Michael Pirie at Green College; Dr Tim Cook at Isis Innovation; John Lange at the Oxford Museum; Harry Lange; Peter Unsworth at the Oxford Mail; Andrew Davies at Barclays; Jackie Wallace-Jones and Ian Hamilton at the Old Bank hotel; and Anita Zabilevska for the photographs.

I would also like to thank the team at Landmark, Lindsey Porter, Mark Titterton, Caroline Wheeler and Stella Porter.

Selected bibliography

Andrews P & Brunner E, The Life of Lord Nuffield, Basil Blackwell, 1955
Balsdon D, Oxford Now and Then, Duckworth, 1970
Carpenter H, The Inklings, Unwin Paperbacks, 1981
Day Lewis C, Fenby C, Anatomy of Oxford, Jonathan Cape, 1938
De Bury R, Philobiblon, Basil Blackwell, 1960
Headlam C, Medieval Towns: Oxford, Dent, 1926
Hobhouse C, Oxford, Batsford, 1948
Norrington ALP, Blackwell's 1879-1979, Blackwell, 1985
Oxford University Handbook, Oxford University Press, 1948
Sherwood J, Pevsner N, Oxfordshire, Penguin, 2001
Sotheby's, Lewis Carroll's Alice, Sale L01912, London, 6.6.2001
Tyack G, Oxford: An architectural guide, Oxford University Press, 1998

Opposite page: **All Souls College**

Oxford

Farrol Kahn

• CONTENTS •

*I*ntroduction

INTRODUCTION

Oxford needs little introduction as it is one of the most famous cities in the world. The university has 750 years of history and from its founding in the thirteenth century, established itself as a centre of academic excellence.

As a resident of Oxford, I have found the university, in spite of the medieval fortified college buildings behind which undergraduates and graduates spend a sheltered scholarly existence, welcoming to the town. The genius of the place responds to anyone who has a love of learning.

TWO FACES OF OXFORD

Oxford is a city of books. The city, which for several hundred years has been under the thumb of the university, has more recently however, achieved an identity of its own through the motor industry, setting it apart from that other ancient university city, Cambridge and bringing prosperity into the city. Although the impact of the industry has lessened, the new Mini is now the only car produced in the city, it has attracted another kind of wheels, with the location of the headquarters of three of the adrenalin-charged Grand Prix motor-racing teams on the outskirts.

The town has also gained from the commercial success of the dons, past and present, who have stepped out of the shadow of the cloister into the world.

Tolkien author of 'Lord of the Rings' is a good example of the old fashioned method of writing books that became bestsellers. Although he disapproved of publicity tours, he nevertheless splurged £47 in 1967 on a black velvet smoking jacket at the local bespoke tailor, the same establishment that had to sue Oscar Wilde to settle his bills for his outrageous outfits. Nowadays, dons set-up businesses at the end of the their lab benches and spin-out companies turn them into millionaires. However, they still nurse suspicions about the outside world, which they believe will rook them, and turn to people like Dr Tim Cook, a leading business incubator who runs Isis Innovations.

'Although Oxford is the most innovative university in the UK with spin-outs', he said, 'it lags behind the US where academics sue the universities for not making them millionaires quick enough.'

GARDENS

Gardening and gardens are also an attraction in Oxford for both gown and town pursue the activity with great enthusiasm. Once a year there is a garden festival under the auspices of the National Gardens Scheme when home owners and colleges open their private gardens to the public on occasions from April to October. There are also the formal gardens and parklands outside the city from the grand Blenheim Palace, where the lake was designed by 'Capability' Brown to Rousham Park House of which Timothy Walker, Superintendent of the University Botanic Garden said:

'It is big and enchanting and the place for gardeners to see before they die'.

AMERICAN INFLUENCE

The American presence at Oxford has become prominent through the closer links with US universities like Princeton and visits of ex-President Clinton, particular since his daughter, Chelsea, was a student at his old college. There have been occasional sightings of Mr Clinton as he bounded out of his hotel across St Giles in his jogging togs towards the Parks or later with a group of reporters in tow when he regaled them with stories of his Rhodes scholarship days. There is talk of a Clinton museum at his old digs in Leckford Road although the exhibits would be minimalist; a mattress on the floor beside a Xerox copier.

HISTORY OF OXFORD

SITE

Oxford lies in a valley between two rivers, the Thames, near its source, and the Cherwell, which join at a spot where the town was first established on an unbroken expanse of wetlands. The rivers were considered to be barriers and would have provided protection for settlements in prehistoric times on the higher and drier valley gravels on Port Meadow and St. Ebbe's, near the centre. The wetlands were good sources of food for hunters providing them with a profusion of game and the agriculturalists would have found the gravel-covered clay soil ideal for cultivation.

Early settlers would have found themselves a secure place open to the north and with transport down and up the River Thames.

EARLY TIMES

The actual name first occurs in the Anglo-Saxon Chronicle for the year 912 and is a derivation from Oxenaforda, a spot where oxen could cross. The ford in question is now believed to be Hinksey Ferry near North Hinksey village and not Folly Bridge, the medieval Grand Pont where there was a causeway early in the twelfth century. Another unusual name, Carfax, is derived from 'quatre fourgs' or 'four ways' from which three main streets descend north, east and west.

The Romans bypassed the city for Dorchester, where they established a garrison town, and it was left to the Danes to put Oxford on the map. This they did in 1010 when it was burnt and eight years later, the great Canute or Knud, King of Denmark and England, held a 'gernot' or Great Council in Oxford where he promised to rule justly. They made it a capital city and his illegitimate son, Harold the Harefoot, was crowned King there.

After the Norman Conquest, the Doomsday Book recorded that half the thousand houses were unoccupied or in ruins and that the town had eight churches and 2,000 inhabitants. The Normans also found traces of its Saxon heritage, St. Michael's Tower, at the north gate in Cornmarket, which the governor, Robert d'Oilly repaired.

MEDIEVAL TIMES

The city's national importance declined for a time until King Henry I built Beaumont Palace (on the site of the present Beaumont Street), which became his favourite residence. Richard I or, as he was known, Richard the Lionheart, conqueror of Saladin and great crusader, was born at the Palace. He and his younger brother King John, who was probably also born there, were the children of Henry II and his wife Eleanor of Aquitaine. Little remains of the Beaumont Palace except a wall between Beaumont Buildings and Walton Street.

Royal favour was shown to the city through the liberal and ample charters granted to the city by both Henry I and Henry II. What is interesting is the link between London and Oxford, which have one and the same custom and law and liberty. The Mayor of Oxford is accorded, and still holds, a special place and privilege at every new royal coronation, as does the Lord Mayor of London.

University

The life of the first British university began as Thomas Becket lay dead by the altar steps at Canterbury Cathedral in 1170. One cannot imagine a more dramatic event for the establishment of a famous institution. Of course, the actual date is uncertain, but around this time foreign-born scholars were driven out of Paris from schools on the Seine because of the English King Henry II's quarrel with the French and Becket.

When Gerald of Wales lectured there in 1186, a large audience of doctors, masters and scholars attended and by the turn of the century, 1200, a body of scholars organised themselves on the lines of the University of Paris.

The student entered at the age of 16 and, like an apprenticeship, his education lasted for seven years. The first degree was a Batchelor of Arts (BA), which was awarded after four years, and the Masters (MA) three years later, was a license to teach in any university in Europe. The course encompassed the Trivium, which was a means of expression of thought through grammar, rhetoric and logic and the Quadrivium. These four subjects included arithmetic, geometry, astronomy and music, to which others were added later, like natural, moral and metaphysical philosophy, tongues (Greek and Hebrew) and history.

There were also courses of study for superior degrees in theology, medicine and law permitted only to BAs and MAs. As members of the university were in effect minor orders of the church, academic robes or gowns were worn, a tradition still carried on today. What is remarkable is that if one stands in the old quadrangle of Schools in the Bodleian, the whole course of the medieval education, which is written in stone, lies before you.

Examination was by public disputation and argument because of the scarcity of writing material. Again, the visitor can tread in the footsteps of the medieval scholar and enter the Divinity School where examinations took place.

Gown vs town

Accommodation was a source of continuous quarrels between the scholars and the townsmen as landlords charged extortionate rents. Eventually the academics banded together to rent or buy 'halls' of their own.

The first serious dispute arose in 1209 when a scholar, practising his archery, accidentally killed a woman in the street. The mayor and burgesses raided lodgings and two clerks were later hanged by the townsmen. The university took fright and dispersed, some to Reading, some to Paris and some to Cambridge, where the sister body was established. The Pope settled the quarrel, through issuing a charter to the university, still in its possession, that required the townsmen to limit their rents and to undertake to pay a small tribute to it forever.

The first step had been taken to impose the University's authority on the town. From this time onwards, townsmen could not arrest a scholar but had to hand him over to the Chancellor, who was also responsible for receiving the tribute, which was put into a university chest. Shortly after, proctors were introduced, whose business was to maintain discipline among the scholars. It was a significant period for the university, as William of Durham, who died in 1249, left it a sum of 310 marks, which the authorities used to purchase what is now University College. Some three decades later, Balliol and Merton were also founded.

Robert Grosseteste, one of the greatest scholars and churchmen, became the first known Chancellor of the University.

St. Scholastica's Day

In 1355, on 10 February, there was a bloody battle between Gown and Town. It started in a tavern appropriately called 'Swindlestock', when the scholars complained of the quality of the wine and a fight ensued. Soon the tocsin was sounded, by ringing the bell of St. Martin in Carfax Tower, which rallied the townsmen. At the same time the bells of St. Mary the Virgin summoned the scholars. A cause for misgiving and jealousy would have been the wealth and rapid growth of the university, which now had six colleges within the narrow walled city. In the end, the academics were no match for the citizens, assisted by hundreds of country-folk, and who together looted and burnt the halls and besieged Merton College for a week. Some 63 scholars were killed, 'The gutter of Brewer's Lane ran with academic blood'.

After the slaughter of 1355, the Chancellor acquired almost total authority, with support of both the Pope and the King, over the trade and independence of the town. They controlled the quality of bread and ale, checked weights and measures, fixed rents, and exercised discipline over citizens and scholars including the authority, if such an instance arose, to hang the Mayor.

On 10 February, every year after until 1825, the Mayor and 62 of the freemen had to attend a service of penance at St. Mary's and offer a penny each on the altar to atone for the scholars slain in the riots.

REFORMATION

Queen Mary I or Bloody Mary, (who reigned from 1553-1558), the daughter of Henry VIII, attempted to reverse the country's turn towards Protestantism and instigated religious persecutions by which she earned her nickname. Almost 300 Protestants were burnt at the stake including Bishops Thomas Cranmer, Nicholas Ridley and Hugh Latimer, who were removed from the Tower of London and placed in custody at Oxford in 1555.

There, these Cambridge men were tried in the Divinity School by a commission from London who denounced them as heretics. Ridley and Latimer were the first to be brought to the stake erected outside Balliol, and, to ease their pain from the fire at their feet, gunpowder was hung about their necks and kindled so that it exploded. It worked for Latimer but not for Ridley, as the gunpowder did not ignite.

Cranmer, who had been in prison for three years and recanted, later joined them in their fate. 'This is the hand that wrote it', he said as he extended his right hand over the flames, 'therefore, it shall suffer first punishment.' He was steadfast as he held it and never cried when the fire reached him. His portrait hangs in the Bodleian.

The Martyrs' Memorial, opposite the west front of Balliol College, was raised in 1841. It was designed by Sir George Gilbert Scott in imitation of the crosses erected by Edward I, in memory of his queen Eleanor, and sometimes is mistaken for the steeple of the sunken church by visitors.

CIVIL WAR

If Elizabeth took Oxford to her heart, Charles I made it his capital in his days of trial during the Civil War, 1642–1646. The university was sympathetic to the Royalist cause while the citizens were less keen because they feared the damage that the enemy could do to the town.

King Charles rode in with his army at the North gate on 29 October 1642, after the indecisive battle at Edgehill 25 miles to the north, and established himself, his ministers, including Ned Hyde, and his court at Christ Church. His two sons and the Princes Rupert and Maurice accompanied him. For the next three and a half years, Oxford was his capital to which he always returned after his campaigns.

The great guns, 26 or 27 pieces with all their carriages, were driven into Magdalen Grove. Here he kept watch over the movements of his troops from Magdalen Tower as they jangled through the quadrangles. He found himself 'at good ease', the place being 'entirely at his devotion' as did his courtiers, who made free with the buttery and the cellars.

Undergraduates enlisted, and erected the fortifications. Trenches were dug in the north of the city, logs hauled across the road at Magdalen to keep out horsemen, and the tower stocked with stones. Merton gardens were a favourite haunt for the courtiers as it was on the safe side of the town with the Thames and Cherwell protecting the south-east. A channel was cut to enable the Cherwell to flood Christchurch Meadows.

At New Inn Hall in January 1643, the mint was set up to which the colleges made presents of their valuable gold, silver and metal plate to be melted down. A crown piece struck at the time called the 'Oxford crown' has, underneath the King's horse, a view of Oxford. One of the colleges that was less than generous with its plate, was Corpus Christi, which still has fine examples from that period today.

New college cloisters housed the ammunition, the Belfry Tower was the powder-mill and wooden drawbridges were made in the 'Schola Rhetoricae' at the Bodleian.

Charles' court at Oxford

The city was unique during the time because of the extraordinary mixture of people of every, rank, disposition and taste.

The ancient colleges and halls thronged with ladies and gentlemen, some of whom felt like fishes out of water as they were obliged to be content with 'a very bad bed in a garret of a baker's house in an obscure street, and one dish of meat a day, and that not the best order, no money and no clothes.'

Soldiers were quartered in the college gates and kitchens and a parliament sat from day to day. There were two parliaments then, one in Westminster and the other in Oxford, and each denied the other's existence.

Yet, amidst the confusion caused by such an influx of people, a courtly pomp was maintained beside the learned and religious society.

The King dined and supped in public and walked in state in Christ Church Meadows, Merton Gardens and the Grove of Trinity.

In July, his Queen, Henrietta Maria, arrived in Oxford from Holland escorted by 2,000 foot soldiers, 1,000 horsemen, six pieces of cannon and two mortars and was a welcome addition to the cause. She established herself at Merton in a room over the archway into the Fellows' Quad, which has since been know as the Queen's Chamber. A passage was constructed from it into Merton hall and from the chapel to the grove and gardens of Corpus, where a door, still traceable, opened in the garden wall and the private way continued to the King in the House.

The city was besieged twice during the war. On the second occasion the Royalists, with only 12 day's provisions left and no hope of aid, surrendered on June 20, 1646. Evidence of the Civil War survives, the street South Parade, in Summertown, which is actually north of North Parade and was the parade ground of the Roundheads during a siege. You can also still see the mounds in College gardens, which were part of the fortifications.

The Queen was induced to leave early on in the war, on 17 April 1644 and never met her husband again. The King left Oxford a couple of months before his surrender, disguised as a servant of Dr John Ashburnham, but was captured six days later.

The university was emptied of its scholars by this time and a cartload of Puritan preachers were sent to teach its depleted members the right principles.

Oliver Cromwell became Chancellor of the university in 1650, received an honorary degree, stopped at All Souls and dined at Magdalen. It was left to Edward Hyde, the Earl of Clarendon, and the King's most trusted advisor, to write the history of the war, and a monument in stone was built in his memory from proceeds of the work.

SEVENTEENTH TO TWENTIETH CENTURIES

A famous figure of the seventeenth century was John Fell. The son of Dean Samuel Fell, he was a student at eleven and eventually himself Dean of Christ Church. He crowned Tom Quad with Wren's Tower, entertained Charles II and James I, expelled the English philosopher John Locke, and patronised with kindness Anthony Wood, untiring student, annalist and backbiter, who wrote his memorable history.

Another diarist, Thomas Hearne, left a gloomy picture during the eighteenth century of early Hanoverian Oxford. College heads were neglectful of business and fond of the bottle. Enthusiasm of all kinds, except for violent politics, was out of fashion and particularly for study, was rare.

Joseph Addison, poet, essayist and founder of the 'Spectator', held his fellowship at Magdalen, William Pitt, the youngest British Prime Minister at 24, was at Trinity and Samuel Johnson brought his fierce, unruly independence to Pembroke. The 'mad and violent' undergraduate developed 30 years later into a leader of contemporary thought and lifted the standards of the age as did John Wesley, whose expulsion from

Oxford, he endorsed. The founder of Methodism taught his godly and exacting discipline to a world 'dead in trespasses and sin'

Adam Smith, the Scottish economist and author of *Wealth of Nations*, went to Balliol in 1740 and William Blackstone, the English Jurist, became one of the glories of All Souls.

During the nineteenth century, Christ Church, under Dean Cyril Jackson, was at the head of reform to introduce an examination system and was crammed from garret to cellar with budding statesmen.

Canning, Peel and Gladstone all made their mark in politics as Prime Ministers, and Robert Peel was the first man to achieve a 'double first' in examinations. It was a great success for Jackson, who had urged all undergraduates to read Homer.

The university also assumed a leading role in religious controversy through the Oxford Movement to revive Catholic tradition in the Anglican Church. John Newman, later, Cardinal, was a leading light in the Movement.

The British Empire was a pre-occupation of the university until the early twentieth century. Benjamin Jowett, Master of Balliol, was prominent in espousing the view that his pupils should govern the world and that the purpose of the Empire was to 'enable Oxford men to do good.' In fact the Indian Institute was established to train civil servants to run India for the British Raj; the means for carrying out their mission – a competent proficiency in Latin and Greek, a knowledge of the rudiments of religion ('rudders') and a comprehensive acquaintance of the history of ancient Greece.

Modern history was relegated to those without the intellectual equip-ment to study the classics and modern languages were suitable only for 'couriers or a foreign clerk or to a gentleman setting out for his first tour of the continent.'

Science was judged to be an interloper at Oxford, to 'stifle the acquirement of knowledge for its own sake', and therefore until the late 1920s, at least a knowledge of Greek was a requirement before studies in it could be undertaken.

COMMERCIAL HISTORY OF THE CITY

The city had a number of trade guilds, which demonstrated its commercial success. Among them were the merchants, the weavers, the cordwainers (shoemakers or workers in Cordovan leather), the glovers, the cooks, the barbers (who dined once a year with the Vice Chancellor) and the most prominent of all, the tailors, who on 23 June walked in procession around the streets accompanied by a band.

'The university found Oxford a busy, prosperous borough and reduced it to a cluster of lodging houses', wrote a scholar, Mr Green.

When the railways arrived, there was opposition from the University, which was concerned about undergraduate disapproval. It bypassed the city and Didcot was established instead as a station on the mainline. Academics did not mind journeys to and from the station in a coach and horses until a branch line was run between the two in 1844.

Small businesses flourished like Frank and Jane Cooper of the High, whose marmalade was so popular that a factory was built to manufacture the product. The rise of the motor industry through the success of a local man, William Morris, accounted for the city's prosperity in the twentieth century.

WILLIAM MORRIS

William Morris, bicycle mechanic, set up his own business at the age of seventeen, in 1894. Unlike his American counterparts, the Wrights, who were flight-obsessed, he was smitten by the motor car. He operated from James Street at the back of his parent's house where he fixed back-pedalling brakes and mended punctures for undergraduates. From the start, he was innovative and a gifted natural engineer, for he was never trained, and seized opportunities whenever they arose.

He built a customised cycle, with a 27-inch frame for a large customer that launched him as a maker of Morris cycles. Within two years, he had extended his interests to include the manufacture of motor cycles and repair of cars, and now had premises in the High Street and had taken a workshop in Longwall, wedged in beside the bastion of the old city wall.

In 1913 he launched a light, sturdily constructed car with a highly efficient engine that was economical to maintain. The **Morris-Oxford** was a two-seater, 8.9 hp car and although not the cheapest on the market, the retail price was £165, it was the most reliable.

The Bullnose Morris, as it became known because of its distinctive shaped radiator, was assembled on a stationary production line in Cowley, a suburb of Oxford. By 1926, the manufacture of the car had moved away from coach building techniques of horse-drawn carriages to the use of an all steel body composed of individual panels pressed from steel strips and a production output of nearly 100,000 cars a year.

The works at Cowley, which are now occupied by the BMW Group, employed some 4,000 men and in the floor space of 81 acres turned out a range from the little Morris Minor to the luxury six-cylinder saloon.

In 1934 an innovation, a moving assembly line was introduced and some 97,000 of the new Morris Eight were produced. In 1938 Morris was created Lord Nuffield. He founded the Nuffield Foundation for medical, social and scientific research and endowed Nuffield College.

The Mini

The Mini, which was only 10ft (3m) long, was the smallest car it manufactured, and one that captured the imagination of the public for over four decades. It was designed by Alex Issigonis.

When the Mini was launched in 1959, it was apparent that Issigonis had taken the William Morris legacy of a lightweight, economical car to heart. It was a car designed around four adults who occupied 80 per cent of the space. To achieve this the engine was installed sideways and the gearbox placed underneath it. There were small wheels to match, placed at the extreme corners to create a large interior.

The Mini anticipated the changing social values of the 1960's and was both a commercial and social success. It was the most successful British car selling 5.3 million models.

Opposite page: The Cathedral at Christ Church

A Walking Tour of Oxford

1

A WALKING TOUR OF OXFORD

Oxford is not as old as London, York, Canterbury, Lincoln and Cambridge, but few cities contain more splendid buildings within a small area. A walking tour, over a couple of hours, will provide the visitor with a good insight into its architecture, university colleges and the old Saxon town. As the route is mainly on the flat with gentle slopes, it can be enjoyed by all age groups.

The tour begins in the oldest street of the city, **St Aldates**, formerly Fish Street, outside **Christ Church**. On the left is Pembroke College, founded in 1614 and named after the then Chancellor of the University, the third Earl of Pembroke. One of its undergraduates was Samuel Johnson or the famous Dr Johnson, who spent an unhappy and brief period there, barely four terms. But he benefited from lectures across the road until his shoes wore out and humiliated by his poverty, he came no more.

CHRIST CHURCH

Standing outside one of the three entrances and looking up, one can see the statue of the founder Cardinal Wolsey and 48 coats of arms of the benefactors. Above is one of Oxford's incomparable architectural gems, **Tom Tower**, which was designed by Sir Christopher Wren in 1681. Although attempts were made to house an observatory in his tower, he refused. Instead it contains a giant bell, called Tom.

Once inside, the visitor is confronted by **Tom Quad**, the grandest and largest quadrangle in Oxford. In the centre of the green velvet lawns is a pool presided over by a statue, known as Mercury. The little fountain has served another purpose when undergraduates who have refused to conform to standards of decency, instead of being debagged – relieved of their trousers – are dipped in the water to cries of 'Put him in Mercury'.

The Hall is the most impressive of the original buildings and is reached by the arch beneath Bodley's bell-tower in the south-east corner. Mount the great stone stair-way that is folded round a column on which rests a most remarkable specimen of fan-vaulting. It was built in 1640 during Dean Samuel Fell's time, by a London stonemason called Smith, some two centuries after the end of the era of fan vaulting. The Dean, a royalist, later died of a broken heart after the execution of King Charles I in 1649.

At the top of the stairs is the finest hall in Oxford with a wide wooden hammerbeam roof and a tall vaulted bay that lights the dais of the high table. The atmosphere and space is similar to when King Henry VIII banqueted here or during the Civil War when King Charles I dined with loyal followers. As in every college, there are portraits assembled on the walls. But here one finds an incomparable collection, hanging from nineteenth-century panelling; a triple portrait by Lely, a profusion of Gainsborough and Reynolds, a Romney of John Wesley, founder of Methodism and a Kneller of John Locke, the philosopher. It is odd that the only figure in a portrait wearing armour is the Quaker, William Penn.

Fans of Alice in Wonderland will find pictures of C L Dodgson (Lewis Carroll) and Alice's father, Dean Liddell.

On the right leaving the hall are steps to the kitchen, a vast chamber with a wooden roof and with the Wolsey coat of arms hanging above the fireplace between two large old turtle shells. As there was no chimney, the smoke travelled up the blackened wall through the open louvre in the middle of the roof.

THE CATHEDRAL

At the foot of the staircase exit into Tom Quad and look for the sign to the cloisters. A door in the north-west corner leads in to the **Cathedral**, which distinguishes Christ Church from other colleges because it also serves as the church of the bishop and his diocese.

Near the site of the Anglo-Saxon church of the nunnery of St Frideswide, it incorporates decorative features from that period, the twelfth century. Parts of the saint's elegantly carved superstructure of her shrine were reconstructed on a new base in the Lady Chapel. There are vestiges of other eras, particularly Norman England and the Victorians. The massive spire, which is one of the oldest in England and crowns the thirteenth-century Norman tower, can be seen from Tom quad or outside in Christ Church meadow.

Looking right, down the nave after entering, there are two features immediately catch the eye; the great Norman columns, Romanesque in their essentials, and the superb lierne vaulted ceiling. Another prominent element is the three arches, the trefoil, in ascending order that emphasise height. The shape of the building is not the usual oblong but almost square and when you walk through, it is full of aisles, chapels and odd corners.

To the left is the north transept or cross-arm of the cruciform, the Latin chapel (circa 1320) and the Lady chapel (circa 1250). The former has a seventeenth-century Vice Chancellor's throne, dark oak stalls and fourteenth-century glass in the north windows. Of interest to readers of Alice in Wonderland is an early Edward Burne-Jones' window illustrating in bright colours, the life of St Frideswide, including the treacle well at Binsey.

The Lady chapel opposite is the result of the thirteenth-century cult of the Virgin Mary and an example of Early English Gothic. It is here that the remains of St Frideswide shrine can be seen. The shrine was smashed on King Henry VIII's orders and dumped down a well where it was found and pieced together.

The window was designed by William Morris and Edward Burne-Jones, the Pre-Raphaelite duo who have another window in the south aisle. Among the tombs lies that of Robert Burton (1639), author of the Anatomy of Melancholy.

Near the south transept, both in the choir aisle and St Lucy's chapel are monuments to cavaliers and others. The transept contains a rare memento, a stained glass window (circa 1347) depicting the murder of Thomas Becket, Archbishop of Canterbury, who opposed his king Henry II. When Cardinal Wolsey opposed King Henry VIII over his divorce to Catherine of Aragon, he was stripped of all his property and the King, ordered all images of Becket to be destroyed. This one strangely survived.

Exiting through the west door, we pass the Deanery and go under Kill Canon tower into the **Peckwater Quad**. The name of the tower derived from the north-easterly draughts that passed through and were deemed to be fatal to the delicate constitutions of canons who lived in Tom Quad. 'Peck', formerly the site of Peckwater Inn, is a good example of Palladian architecture and its wide staircases and tall rooms are a model of what an Oxford quad should be. Before the World War I, this quad like many others was gravelled rather than grassed over, which became the fashion. The library, which was designed by the amateur

Tom Quad, the largest quadrangle in Oxford with Sir Christopher Wren's Tom Tower in the background.

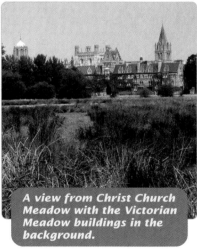

A view from Christ Church Meadow with the Victorian Meadow buildings in the background.

architect, Dr George Clarke, a fellow of All Souls, favoured Baroque, so the façade is one of the grandest for such an institution and has giant Corinthian columns.

The building like others at the time was meant to be open on the ground due to the fear of damp, while the books would be kept on the drier floors above. However, such a scheme was defeated by the bibliophilic academics and the ground floor had to be enclosed to house the overflow of volumes.

Enter **Canterbury Quad** and exit through its monumental triumphal arch though visitors interested in paintings may wish to enter the picture gallery to the right. It has works by Tintoretto, Van Dyck, Leonardo da Vinci, Michaelangelo and the portrait of King Henry VIII by Hans Holbein. An unusual item is a painting of a butcher shop that used to hang in the kitchen. It could have been obtained by the House for sentimental reasons as the founder, Cardinal Wolsey was the son of a butcher.

Merton Street, a cobbled thoroughfare, lies straight ahead and on your left is **Oriel Square** with the college of the same name on the left.

One of its alumni was Cecil Rhodes who endowed Rhodes Scholarships, which have brought to Oxford 32 Americans, 30 students from the Commonwealth and two from Germany every year since.

As we proceed to **Merton**, we pass **Corpus Christi** on our right, which is the smallest undergraduate college, with a pelican sundial. Among its alumni were General Oglethorpe, founder of the State of Georgia in the US, John Keble and Sir Isaiah Berlin.

Merton College

Merton is a small, wealthy college and its statutes set the example for most colleges. Before the rules were laid down, an individual selfishly pursued his own studies without thought of loyalty, affection and of being service to the other members. It was the founder Walter de Merton, Bishop and Lord Chancellor of England who in 1264 was the first to express the true idea of the collegiate system.

'A college is justly defined, not as the mere recipients of a benefaction, not as the buildings in which such may live together, but as a self-governing corporate community with common rule, common life, common property, common end'.

By this test Merton is the oldest college rather than University and Balliol, which obtained their statutes later. Also it is the only one of the three that has retained its founder's buildings.

A view of Merton College from the Broad Walk

MERTON COLLEGE

Enter though the gatehouse, above which is the tower that dates from 1418, when King Henry V gave permission for the protective wall at the top of the battlements. Both the King and the founder have statues in the gate-tower. The obvious feature of the college is that it is not built on the quadrangular model which came to the fore a century later when New College was established. The buildings developed piecemeal. The doors of the gatehouse are original as is the former Warden's lodgings to the left of the front quad.

The Hall is straight ahead and is basically thirteenth-century, and although it was reconstructed in the eighteenth and nineteenth century, the west wall is genuine. The door is extraordinary with wrought-iron work of a scroll design. Another interesting element is the gateway into the Fellows Quad built by Warden Fitzjames in 1497 with an excellent lierne-vault and ornamental carvings of the signs of the Zodiac. As you enter, the classical frontispiece at the centre of the south range catches the eye. It is an impressive classical motif.

Return to the **Front Quad** and turn left through the passageway past the ancient sacristy and treasury into **Mob Quad** and in the south and west sides on the first floor is the library. These buildings, as well as the Quad, whose name is obscure, are the oldest in Oxford.

The library which is modelled on the late thirteenth-century system found at the Sorbonne in Paris, has single-light windows illuminating spaces between the reading stalls in which chained books were kept. In the room beyond is a collection of cartoons by caricaturist and author of *Zuleika Dobson*, Max Beerbohm. Outside, enter the chapel at the opposite end of Mob Quad.

The building is the first and the largest of the college chapels and has a spacious and exhilarating interior. The thirteenth-century glass is of note, particularly the intricate tracery of the east window and the crystalline beauty of the transepts. The lectern is of spun brass and three of the five arches of the screen, set up in the crossing, were designed by Sir Christopher Wren. The base of the bell tower, which is a good example of the perpendicular style, was completed in 1450 and contains eight bells.

Exit the college and turn left into a passageway between Merton and Corpus Christi, called Merton Grove to continue the walk. The Grove leads to **Christ Church meadow**, an area of delightful walks, including one along the Cherwell river. However, take the first left in Deadman's Walk, which was a strip of land inside the city wall, along which the Jewish community carried their dead to the cemetery. This is now the site of the gardens. The name is not derived, as some guides will tell visitors, from the beheading of a Cavalier officer there.

Before turning into Rose Lane on the left, there is a plaque to James Sadler, the English balloonist who ascended in a hot air balloon in 1784, two years after the exploits of the French pioneers, the Montgolfier brothers. Off the Lane is the **University of Oxford Botanic Garden**. A handsome Baroque gateway is at the entrance. Over the arch is a bust of the Earl of Danby who gifted the land, and in niches at the sides are statues of Charles I and Charles II. The Botanic garden is the oldest in the UK and has been continually cultivated for almost 400 years.

May Day follies

This end of the High, as locals call the street, is known for its student frolics, particularly in the early hours of May Day, when a choir serenades crowds below and undergraduates quaff champagne and jump into the river off Magdalen Bridge.

Punts, those peculiar narrow, flat-bottomed boats that are propelled by long poles, are found for hire at this end of the riverside as they are under Folly Bridge near Christ Church. From Rose Lane, there is a good view of Magdalen from the south. It is built on the former site of the thirteenth-century St John's Hospital, which was incorporated in 1458 into the college when founded by William Waynflete.

MAGDALEN COLLEGE

The eye is immediately drawn to the beautifully proportioned tower that strikes one with awe. This was described as 'The most absolute building in Oxford' by King James I. The battlemented wall protects the exquisite buildings inside and the college stands aside, aloof from the medieval town whose boundaries were marked by the Eastgate hotel on the left.

The college has moved on its axis as the entrance was once through an impressive gate along **Longwall** on the west side. Now entry is under the low nineteenth-century gateway that leads into St John's Quad enclosed by straggling building. To the right are adapted buildings of the former hospital and in the corner the open-air pulpit where a sermon is still preached every year on St John the Baptist.

The other buildings, from the right anticlockwise, are the ante-chapel; the Muniment Tower; the Founder's Tower, with finely carved bay windows and the President's Lodgings. Detached is the Grammar Hall, which was built in 1614 and rebuilt in 1828. It was established to educate the choristers. On the left is **St Swithin's Quad** (1880–4) and beyond the Longwall buildings, which are wonderfully fitted in oak.

Enter under the **Muniment Tower**, where documents were kept and immediately to the right is the door into the ante-chapel with its graceful arches. The chapel doorway is carved with angels and the interior is covered by rib-vaulting. However, although the proportions are good and the architectural form is pleasing, there is little inside that is old because the interior was gutted in 1830s and the old embellishments sold.

The one treasure that the chapel has always preserved has been its music and its choral services are famous in this musical city. So keen are the choirmasters on the quality that one actually kidnapped a talented poor boy from Malmesbury to serve as a chorister. Oliver Cromwell, a lover of music, took a fancy to the fine organ in the chapel and had it delivered to Hampton Court.

Continued on Page 24

The garden began as a collection of 3,000 plants, including medicinal herbs, for the seventeenth-century physicians and has evolved into the most diverse in the world in just 4.5 acres (1.82 hectares). The layout represents the ideal prevailing at the time; the geometrical pattern of plots and paths, the fountains and the statues that might have been found in the Tudor and Stuart era in every college garden. Of the avenue of yews that were trimmed into the shape of giants, only one remains at the far end of the central path.

Through a combination of beauty – the views of towers are spectacular from the water garden – and efficiency, it holds its own with the older one at Padua (1545) and the younger Physic garden at Chelsea in London (1673). The yellow Oxford Ragwort (Senecio Squalida) grown here by the first gardener, Jacob

Bobart, from seeds collected on the slopes of Mt Etna, Italy, has spread all over the UK.

The garden is known worldwide as having the best collection of euphorbias. There are nine glasshouses in which flourish ferns, orchids, lotuses, palms and bananas, but the water lettuce, a pernicious weed has failed to grow. Other features include bog and rock gardens, two large herbaceous borders and a walled garden.

Opposite page: Two views of Magdalen Tower, top from the water garden, bottom, with the 19th century Magdalen College Bursary building and Botanic garden conservatory.

Leave the chapel through the door, into the cloisters reminiscent of Eton, dominated by a single entrance tower known as the **Founder's Tower**. Look up at the beautiful vaulting and proceed to the left.

PARKLANDS OF MAGDALEN

Continue along to the north side of the cloister where there is a fine view of the hall, chapel, and the belltower, behind. Slip through a passage onto the lawns in front of the New Building of 1733, which has an aspect of an elongated Georgian country house. It stands alone amid the largest parklands, some 100 acres (40.5 hectares) and on the edge of the Grove with its herd of deer.

To the east are the water-meadows surrounded by the branches of the Cherwell and Addison's Walk, which was named after the English poet, dramatist and politician, who founded the Spectator. During March, flowers proliferate and in late April and early May at the far end, bloom many fritillaries or snakeshead, a bell-shaped plant. In spite of such beautiful surroundings, Edward Gibbon, who lived in the New Building, was disgruntled with his period at the college.

Return from the bridge over the river, moving south towards the gabled group of buildings by the kitchen which date to the thirteenth century and belonged to the hospital. Enter the cloister again in the middle of the east side and turn left to the Hall which was restored in 1902. It has a very fine Jacobean screen (with fluted Corinthian columns, circa 1605) and the splendid linen-fold panelling of the rest of the hall is even older. In the middle of the wall above the High Table are

seventeen ornate, carved Renaissance panels, one with the figure of King Henry VIII and another five from the legend of Mary Magdalen. The oriel window depicts seventeenth-century portraits of King Charles I and his Queen Henrietta Maria.

Retrace the steps and emerge once again in the High. It is one of the world's great streets with a panorama of impressive buildings. Colleges and churches that are offset by Georgian and more modest houses are exposed by a wide curve.

Final Schools

Undergraduates wear gowns for lectures and for examinations. Men wear subfusc (dark suits) with white bow ties and mortar boards, while women also dress in dark skirts, white blouses with black ties, stockings and shoes. Graduates, examiners and invigilators similarly wear academic dress.

'Road surfacing' ceremonies are held behind the Examination Halls in the cobbled Merton Street after the Final Schools during which undergraduates celebrate with champagne, confetti and other high jinks under the watchful eyes of the bull-dogs or university police. The undergraduates return in July for their oral examinations or vivas.

On the left are the **Examination Halls**, where lectures are given during term and at the beginning of June they become the scene of degree examinations or 'Final Schools' as they are known.

QUEEN'S COLLEGE

Opposite the Examination Halls is **Queen's College,** which makes a dramatic impact on the High through its temple-like cupola resting on arches supported by pairs of Doric columns. The dome, which shelters a statue of the wife of George II, Queen Caroline, who gave the blessing for rebuilding in the 1700s, is a centrepiece with two tall, pedimented wings on either side. The patron of the college was an earlier Queen, Edward III's Queen Philippa, whose chaplain Robert de Eglesfield was the founder in 1341. It was called the Queen's partly as a counterpart to her husband's, the King's Hall at Cambridge (later Trinity College).

The layout of the **Front Quad** is French in character, apparently modelled after the Palais de Luxembourg in Paris, with an open-ended courtyard screened off from the street by the first classical façade in an Oxford college. The Quad is the grandest piece of English Baroque in the city and like Magdalen the original entrance was from another part, the north side. Both Christopher Wren and Nicholas Hawksmoor have had a hand in the architecture.

The Hall is on the left and the chapel on the right of the north range, which has a strong resemblance to Wren's Chelsea Hospital in London. It is designed in classical style and throughout has a barrel-vaulted ceiling. Above the entrance is a gallery with an ornamental iron balcony, which has been used by visitors as a viewing platform to observe members of the college at their meals.

College customs

The unusual feature of the High Table is the seating which was supposed to accommodate only thirteen members, the Provost seated in the middle with the fellows on either side of him, similar to the Twelve Apostles. Another custom is to bring a boar's head to High Table at Christmas to commemorate an undergraduate who claimed to have killed that animal through thrusting a copy of Aristotle down its throat. On New Year's Day the Bursar gives each Fellow a needle and thread, the origin of which is a pun on Eglefield's name, *aiguille et fil.*

The chapel is entered via a tiny ante-chapel through a splendid wooden screen carved by Grinling Gibbons. It is of an admirable size and has one of the most ecclesiastical interiors of the seventeenth and eighteenth centuries in England.

The library is outstanding and has been described as a noble structure with a gorgeous interior. It is comparable to Wren's superb library at Trinity College, Cambridge and therefore has been ascribed to him. Like the one at Christ Church, it rested on a loggia that was closed in 1841 to increase book space. There is an outstanding plaster ceiling with dainty Rococo decoration and it is lit by tall round-headed windows which provide the large rectangular room with a feeling of space and light, unlike the scholarly gloom that is reminiscent of other, older college libraries.

The bookcases, placed traditionally at right angles, are richly carved and each pair provide a secluded bay for study. Grinling Gibbons' carvings are scattered about the bookcase-ends, completing the effect of lavish luxury. Between the doorways, are niches for statues of Queen Henrietta Maria, Robert Eglesfield, Edward II, Queen Philippa and Charles I.

Visitors who have time should go along the walled passage that runs westwards from the south of the library to the old college brewery and turn left into **Nunn's Garden**. It is an oasis behind the old houses of the High.

UNIVERSITY COLLEGE

On the opposite side of the street, a little further up are the curved front and two gate-towers of **University College** or Univ as it is more concisely called. The buildings are just three centuries old as, when it was rebuilt, all the original structures were demolished. The style is of the late Gothic used more boldly and successfully at Oriel and Wadham and the most distinctive feature is the range of small, fussy gables on the roofline. The statue over the main gate, facing the High is of Queen Anne (1709).

Enter the Front Quad and on the opposite side facing is another statute of James II in Roman dress. Univ was reputedly founded by Alfred The Great (849–99), but its endowment dates from 1280 when a small society of 4 masters applied for money bequeathed by William of Durham to establish a college.

Across the Quad towards the centrepiece, there are two small entrances, the Hall to the right and the Chapel to the left. The Chapel has suffered from remodelling by Sir

Gilbert Scott, particularly of the roof. The dominant elements are the stained glass and the woodwork. Abraham van Linge's work is rich in colour and exuberant in the depiction of stories in glass. Notable too are the seventeenth-century stalls and screen, which has fine carvings similar in quality to those in Trinity Chapel.

The proportions of the Hall were spoilt when it was lengthened in 1904 through the addition of two extra bays on the west.

Nearby is the **Shelley Memorial**, which was originally intended for the Protestant Cemetery, Rome, where he is buried.

The Shelley Memorial

Lady Shelley presented the lifesize marble sculpture, where the poet is laid out like a dead fish on a fishmonger's slab, to Univ in 1893. He lies under a dome specially designed for the monument. His undergraduate days were shortlived for he was sent down or expelled after only six months in the college. He wrote a pamphlet on 'The Necessity of Atheism', which was distributed to all heads of houses and then steadfastly refused to admit it as his own.

The Shelley Memorial is also of great scientific interest because it was the site of the former house of Robert Boyle, who assisted by Robert Hooke, conducted experiments with the air pump that resulted in the law named after him. Boyle's Law played an important part in the development of aviation and a

An elaborate sundial designed by Sir Christopher Wren embellishes the Codrington library

plaque on the other side on the High commemorates his work.

ALL SOULS COLLEGE

Cross the High again and enter **All Souls**, which has always been unique among Oxford and Cambridge colleges as it alone preserved the medieval habit of admitting graduates only of the higher academic distinction. It is a college of Fellows and one, the learned Chichele Professor of Modern History, Sir Charles Oman, is reported to have said that if he came up against a question he could not answer, there was no need for him to look it up, for he was sure to meet someone who knew all about it in the Common Room or at dinner. One of the brightest intellects of the twentieth century, Sir Isaiah Berlin was elected at the age of 23. Another from an earlier age was Christopher Wren.

History of All Souls

The college of All Souls of the Faithful Departed, which is its full title is the greatest of all war memorials and is dedicated to those who had fallen in the Hundred Years War, fought between France and England, during 1337 to 1453.

It was founded by Henry Chichele (pronounced Chitcheley), Archbishop of Canterbury and his King, Henry VI, in 1438 and unlike other smaller colleges, it has a large and magnificent Chapel, also a chantry foundation like New College. Here the members were required to pray for the souls, especially of those killed in Henry V's wars in France.

Chichele, who was a New College man, copied the plans of his alma mater. Here too there is the gateway tower through which one enters, an enclosed quad – the Front Quad – and a T-shaped chapel in perpendicular gothic. Both the latter and hall are ranged along north side and in the two-storied residential range there are independent and separate staircases. The students slept in a dormitory of four beds and each had a study cubicle. But it is in the library that All Souls differs and triumphs over New College.

Two statues of the founders are in the front of the four-storied gate tower. Proceed across the quad to the chapel that fills the north range and has the mark of Christopher Wren, who was a fellow and reckoned that it was his best work. Upon entry the T-form is obvious and the interior is a total work of great craftsmanship, for it is rich in decorative woodwork and plasterwork. The roof, which is original, is shallow having splendid hammerbeams with angels.

The original reredos behind the altar is marvellous and over it is a marquetry representation of a sunburst which is framed by delicate, limewood carvings of fruit and flowers. Some suggest it is the handiwork of one of the greatest wood-carvers in England, Grinling Gibbons. Other woodwork was carried out by the talented Arthur Frogley and is complemented by the plasterwork on the coved ceiling with panels featuring fruit and flowers in high relief.

An interesting feature is the vaulted undercroft below the eastern side of the chapel that contains two fine statues, of Henry VI and the founder, which date from the time of the foundation and were once displayed on the gate tower.

Through a passage nearby enter the North Quad and the architect Nicholas Hawksmoor's territory, for both the quadrangle and the library are his design. His dramatic signature is characterised by the twin pinnacle towers in mock-gothic which lift the spirits and fire the imagination, and are worthy of a pupil of Christopher Wren.

Codrington Library at All Souls

The **Codrington Library** which adjoins them is one of his greatest works. It was named after a fellow who had made his money out of sugar from Barbados, and commissioned a building to house his large collection of books. At the time, the hall and the chapel formed a single side and Dr George Clarke decided to balance them with a library as big as a cathedral.

Hawksmoor continued with the Gothic style in the exterior but provided the building with a classical interior. Unlike other libraries in Oxford, it was the first to be placed on the ground floor and has bookcases along the walls, enhancing its spaciousness. A splendid feature is the large Venetian window at the east and west ends, which create a wonderful effect of light and air. Among its treasures is a large collection of original drawings by Christopher Wren. There are two commanding marble statues, one of the benefactor Christopher Codrington in Roman dress and the other of Sir William Blackstone, seated on a throne. He was a famous English jurist whose commentaries influenced American law during the period of the Declaration of Independence.

Hawksmoor was also responsible for the interior of the Hall, which was set at right angles to the east wall of the chapel. Of particular note is the Buttery, a vaulted oval room, where the fellows take their lunch.

ST MARY'S CHURCH

Out of All Souls, we turn right into the High and pause outside **St Mary's Church**, which is easily recognised through the south porch with its twisted pillars and curved pediment that breaks into pretty scrolls. The angels heads were hacked off by Cromwell's troops as they were considered to be too popish.

It is the university church dating from 1460 and has been put to all sorts of odd uses, including trials and disputations. Until the Sheldonian Theatre was built, it served both as a church and a theatre, and as a venue for degree-giving ceremonies. It is also the place where, for 500 years until 1854, the Mayor took an oath to keep privileges of the University intact. The church's striking features are the tower (circa 1280) and the spire (1320).

THE BODLEIAN COMPLEX

Enter Catte Street between the church and All Souls and you will arrive at a remarkable group of buildings, the Bodleian complex. It is the heart of the historic university and has been described by Sir Nikolaus Pevsner, as 'unique in the world, or, if that seems too hazardous a statement, it is certainly unparalled at Cambridge'. The first

to delight the eye is the **Radcliffe Camera** or Library as it was known earlier, which is as grand and perfect a building as any in Oxford. Crowned by a dome, it is an impressive work by the architect, James Gibbs, and the first round library that was constructed in England, constructed in 1749. The ochre-coloured stone, a distinctive feature, comes from Burford, a beautiful town outside Oxford.

The circular domed building gives the impression of a Roman mausoleum, which was the original concept, for the ground floor was open as was the custom of libraries at the time and the public could walk in and see the life-size statue of Dr John Radcliffe. He was a generous benefactor of the university and a graduate of Univ. whose skill as a doctor had secured him the post of court physician and whose wit had deprived him of it. He offended William III through his remark that the dropsical monarch would not have his two legs for his two kingdoms.

There is a superb feeling of light and space in the building which is enhanced by decorative plasterwork, particularly the dome. The public cannot gain access to the building except as part of a tour arranged by the Bodleian. However, one can enter the old **Congregation House**, attached to the University Church opposite the Radcliffe Camera. The ground floor has served for deliberative and degree-conferring meetings since 1320 and now is a coffee house. The upper floor housed the first university library in 1412.

For visitors, this is the closest one will get to the cradle of the university. From the outside, the building looks like a chapel and during its time has been the archive room, containing the charters and deeds, as well as serving as a repository for powder and matches during the Civil War.

Under the vaulted chamber, one may find refreshment or lunch. Later you may climb the stairs of St Mary's tower for the best view of Oxford.

BRASENOSE COLLEGE

Enter the Square again and left is **Brasenose College** or BNC as it is known colloquially, which is the only college in Oxford or Cambridge to have its eponymous totem within its walls. In the place of honour in the Hall hangs an ancient bronze knocker or door-handle, consisting of a face with a broad and prominent nose and a movable ring between the teeth, dating from the first half of the twelfth century.

Like Univ., money from William of Durham was used to purchase a corner tenement at Brasenose Lane and Radcliffe Square in 1253, where twelve Masters of Arts settled. Consequently, the college is on the site of the oldest possession of the university for the purposes of education.

THE BODLEIAN LIBRARY

To the right, past the Radcliffe Camera, along Catte Street, one will find the finest temple to Western book culture and the oldest teaching, examination and ceremonial rooms. The first building on the left is often mistaken for a college but instead is the **Bodleian Library**, one of the most famous institutions in the world. Enter under the gate tower through the great oak doors that date from about 1620. These are painted with the royal arms of the Prince of Wales, the university and all the colleges founded at that date.

Once inside the Schools quad, turn back and look at the biggest frontispiece with five orders of columns, starting with Tuscan and followed upwards by Doric, Ionic, Corinthian and Composite. On the fourth storey is a sculptural group showing King James I – the wisest fool in Christendom – seated under a canopy and to his left is Fame and on his right, the kneeling university. The panel was in commemoration of his visit three years earlier.

The Quad was the largest and most impressive architectural work undertaken for university teaching at the time. Looking around, one will see that every little door has a Latin name above it, denoting the names of the schools or lecture rooms to which they gave access: Moral philosophy (law) Grammar and History (Greek), Metaphysics (arithmetic and geometry), Logic (astronomy), Music (rhetoric) and natural philosophy (anatomy and medicine).

This was first a centre of teaching but by stealth the university's monstrous collection of books ousted everything in sight. Floor after floor was taken over by volumes until the whole place was solid with books. The last bastion to fall was the examination room in the 1880s.

The buildings were faced throughout by Headington ashlar stone, which was in abundant supply only a few miles away from the centre of Oxford. The most dramatic range is in the west with the Gothic fantasy design which is the **Proscholium**, or Arts End built in 1612. This is a vestibule to the fabulous Divinity School. The Proscholium now houses the shop that has a rich collection of memorabilia and gifts and

serves as the entrance to the library. It is part of an H-shaped building which is linked to the other part by the library or Duke Humfrey library as it is known.

HISTORY OF THE BODLEIAN

SCHOLA GRAMMATICAE ET HISTORIAE

A door in the Schools Quad painted over with the subject taught in that lecture room

Sir Thomas Bodley (1545–1613), a scholar and diplomat, educated at Magdalen, refounded and enlarged the University library, which had been stripped of its books, either by scholars who did not return volumes they borrowed or by commissioners of Edward VI appointed to reform the university, who destroyed or sold them. In the 1556 Convocation, it was even decided to sell as timber the empty shelves and stalls from Duke Humfrey's library.

During his career, Sir Thomas never forgot the empty room because he believed like the thirteenth century bibliophile Richard de Bury, that a 'library is more precious than all wealth'. When later he returned to Oxford he wrote to the university offering to restore the place at his own expense, an offer that was accepted. He had married a rich widow, whose husband's fortune had been made in pilchard fishing. He set about his task by acquiring collections of books through donations from benefactors like Sir Walter Raleigh and by employing a bookseller to procure books on the Continent. One of the coups of the latter was the purchase of a new copy of Don Quixote in 1607, which is still in the library. He also appointed a librarian, Thomas James, and it was officially opened in 1603 by King James I. As such, it was the first public library in Europe.

An important achievement was to obtain an agreement with the Stationers' company to give the Bodleian a copy of every book they published. The arrangement was a precursor of the Copyright Acts, by which a copy of every book published has to be presented to the library and the British Library.

To ensure that the library would not be ruined again by a lack of books, he specified that no book could be borrowed but had to be read in the library. This stricture was tested when, Charles I tried to borrow D'Aubigne's History - an account of King Henry IV's court and camp life. His request, like Cromwell's, was refused.

Another contribution made by Sir Thomas was to build the east wing of the library, the Arts End, over the Proscholium when there was 'more

need of a library for the books than of books for the library'. He also conceived the idea of rebuilding the Schools Quad and when he was laid to rest in Merton Chapel, the first stone was laid.

John Selden

Eventually the Bodleian would take the form of an H when the Selden wing was built to house the collection of books of John Selden, the distinguished orientalist and jurist, which more than doubled the size of the library. When Seldon's books were sorted, his spectacles were found and Anthony Wood, the antiquary, who helped to carry the books upstairs was given a pair.

Of all the buildings in the Schools, the H-shaped west range is the most magnificent. On the ground floor, the Proscholium leads into the masterpiece of Gothic architecture, the **Divinity School** (1488), which was the University's first examination room. It has been described as the most beautiful room in Europe and the vaulted ceiling is unparalled. Oral examinations were carried out here. The professor of theology would sit between the examiner and the undergraduate.

Enter the adjoining room, the **Convocation House** (1647), which was built at right angles to the Divinity School. It was the meeting place for the University's supreme legislative body. Two features are the richly embellished wood panelling that extends halfway up the wall and the stone, fan vault ceiling. The furnishings have virtually remained unaltered since the seventeenth century when it was used by the House of Commons as a meeting place during the Civil War and when London was stricken by the plague.

Return to the Proscholium, for the pièce de résistance above. Enter into the Arts End, a long, light room, with a timber beam roof, an impressive feature of the whole library. The two-storied bookshelves introduced by Sir Thomas, immediately catch the eye as does the artificial lighting and netting over the windows to protect the books from the sunlight. The effect is dramatic.

The Duke Humfrey's section was named after the Duke of Gloucester, younger brother of King Henry V, whose collection of some 281 manuscripts was gifted to the University and required a new building to house them. At one time, illuminated books were chained to the lecterns and had to be read in a standing position.

At the far end is Selden End, built in 1637 and reached through a rounded arch. It is lit by a fifteenth-century stained-glass panel showing penance of King Henry II after the murder of St Thomas Becket and contains reference books on topographical and antiquarian subjects among others.

Exit and stand in the middle of Schools from which one will be able to view the Radcliffe Camera through one archway and note the alignment of the archways with those of the Clarendon building through to the bust of Sir Thomas on the New Bodleian.

Deluge of books

In an effort to stem the tide of books that pour in at about the rate of 100 volumes a day, occupying 107 miles of shelves and totalling almost 7 million, an underground store was created beneath Radcliffe Square at the end of the nineteenth century and a major extension, the New Bodleian was built.

Enter the North archway that leads to the Clarendon Quad, which is bounded by Catte Street, the Old Bodleian, the Clarendon building and the Sheldonian Theatre. The buildings which have been in constant use since the eighteenth century are a popular venue for Heads of State, royalty and international visitors to the university. Here the work of pupil and master, Hawksmoor and Wren, stand side by side through their creations.

THE CLARENDON BUILDING

The **Clarendon Building** which was built to house the Oxford University Press, was partly financed from the profits of the Earl of Clarendon's (1609–74) posthumous bestseller, *History of the Great Rebellion and the Civil Wars in England*.

Hawksmoor designed it as a grand classical ceremonial entrance to the central university area. There are four giant Tuscan columns and the roof is decorated with statues of the nine muses: history, music, dance, comedy, tragedy, mime, astronomy, epic and lyric poetry. The statue of Clarendon, who was an adviser to

Charles II and Chancellor of the University, stands in a niche facing west.

THE SHELDONIAN

Wren's early work, **the Sheldonian**, which was his first public building, was constructed in 1666 on a D-shaped plan like the ancient Roman theatre of Marcellus in Rome. It arose from the need for a more suitable setting than St Mary's for important secular functions. You can see the Roman theatre in its stepped tiers of seats and clear sightlines. The venue, which is still used as a ceremonial hall as well as a concert hall, was named after Gilbert Sheldon, archbishop of Canterbury, who provided funds for its construction. He deplored the buffoonery that accompanied the annual Encaenia that was conducted within the consecrated walls of St Mary's.

The interior of the Sheldonian is delightful with its painted ceiling and curious boxes, pulpits and galleries that make it an oddity amongst theatres in the world, and has a seating capacity of up to 1,500 people. A memorable feature is the curved end of the building with its railing and herms, pillars topped by Roman heads.

The walk ends here. For those visitors whose appetite for books has been whetted, a stroll across Broad Street or the Broad into the famous bookshop, Blackwells, will satisfy even the most voracious.

There is also an opportunity of forming a permanent link with the Bodleian through becoming a Friend. Details available from email: fob@bodley.ox.ac.uk . ☎01865 277022/234 and Bodleian Library, Oxford, OX1 3BG.

Above: The Sheldonian Theatre an early example of Sir Christopher Wren's work

2

Look out for Architectural details such as this winged angel at the entrance to Magdalen College

ARCHITECTURAL SNAPSHOTS

Everything in and about Oxford is near enough to undertake a personalised tour anytime. Mix and match from the places detailed here, many of which are within walking distance of the City centre, a few will require transport. If you wish to visit colleges, schedule your walk for the afternoons when they usually admit visitors. The asterisks indicate: *** unmissable; ** visit if at all possible; *well-worth a visit; no asterisk – visit if time permits.

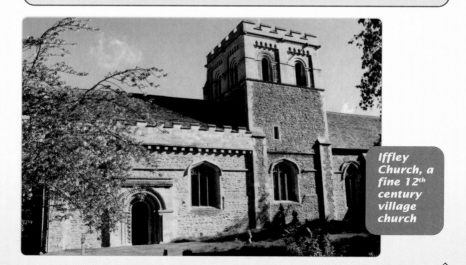

Iffley Church, a fine 12th century village church

All Saints Church (1706-8)

It was designed by Dean Aldrich of Christ Church in Renaissance style and the tower is one of the most successful in Oxford as the steeple sits boldly on it. Built on the site of a medieval church where Shakespeare stood godfather to the dramatist Sir William Davenant, who was rumoured to be his son. Now it is the library of Lincoln College.

**All Souls College (1438)

The buildings have the stamp of three distinguished architects, Nicholas Hawksmoor, Sir Christopher Wren and Dr George Clarke, Fellow of All Souls. Of particular note are Hawksmoor's Codrington Library and twin towers, the Wren sundial, Clarke's oval stone buttery with classic vaulting and the reredos in the chapel.

*Ashmolean(1841-8)

It is the work of the scholarly architect Professor Charles Cockrell. The Ashmolean together with Queen's College and the Radcliffe Camera are considered to be the best large classical buildings in the city. In all, it comprises a museum (having absorbed the collection of curiosities of Elias Ashmole originally kept in the Old Ashmolean in Broad Street), an art gallery and a modern languages faculty, the Taylorian Institute. This Roman-Greek revival is a distinct challenge to the Gothic style of the Randolph Hotel opposite.

Balliol College (1263-8)

Little survives of the original buildings and it has been rebuilt mainly in the nineteenth century. It has the longest façade of any Oxford college, stretching along St Giles and Broad Street.

Blackfriars (1921-9)

A Dominican priory, which is a permanent private hall with an inscription tablet by Eric Gill over the entrance. Both Dominicans and Franciscans (Grey Friars) were powerful elements in the University from early in the thirteenth century through their schools and libraries. Dun Scotus and William Ockham were trained by them and Roger Bacon joined them. While here, the friars also lost their taste for austere living and at one time, lived in the Royal Beaumont Palace.

***Blenheim (1705-1725)

The palace at Woodstock is certainly worth a visit because of the building which was designed by John Vanbrugh and the park, one of the finest pieces of landscape in the UK.

Boars Hill

Only some four miles from the centre, the area offers spectacular views of the spires and towers below on one side and of the Berkshire Downs on the other. Also good for walking and rambling. The Oxford Preservation Trust offers a selection of three walks on Boars Hill. For a brochure that includes a map, contact them at their office, 10 Turn Again Lane, Oxford, OX1 1QL. Telephone 242918. (See entry, Poets and Authors)

***Bodleian Library (1602)

If you only have limited time in the city you should come here. Take a special tour as it will enable you to see inside the two jewels of the library, the Duke Humfrey's on the first floor, which was the original part open to readers in 1488 and the splendid Radcliffe Camera.

***Botanic Garden (1621)

The University's Botanic or physic garden has three gateways built by Nicholas Stone, which represent variations on the Roman triumphal arch. Statues of Charles I and Charles II occupy niches and the founder of the garden Lord Danby, is in a cartouche at the top of the main gate.

Brasenose College (1509)

The name derives from a brass door knocker in the shape of a lion's head and was originally written Brazen Nose Hall or BNC.

Bridge of Sighs (1913-6)

Sir Thomas Jackson designed the bridge over New College Lane, using the Renaissance idea of a covered bridge to link parts of Hertford College.

Campion Hall (1896)

A permanent private hall run by the Society of Jesus and is the only example of Sir Edward Lutyens' work in Oxford.

*Canal (1790)

The Oxford Canal towpath which begins at Hythe Bridge Street is a hidden attraction of the city and during the three-mile walk, the visitor is taken from the former coal wharves past the junction of the Thames, the Victorian suburbs of Jericho, the water meadows, to the village green at Wolvercote. Besides the many houseboats moored on its banks, one of the interesting landmarks en route is St Barnabas' Church, which was inspired by Torcello Cathedral near Venice. In his book, *Jude the Obscure*, Thomas Hardy mentions the church in the guise of St Silas and Jericho as Beersheba. A good companion to the walk is *Our Canal in Oxford* by Davies and Robinson.

Carfax

Junction of four main streets in the town (Cornmarket, Queen Street, St Aldates and the High). Two notable landmarks are the nineteenth-century Town Hall on the corner of the High and St Aldates by Henry Hare, and the fourteenth-century tower of St Martin, the only part of the church which remains. The tower offers a view of the city.

Castle (1071)

Little remains of the Norman Castle built by Robert d'Oilly except St George's Tower (Paradise Street) and the earth mound or motte (in New Road).

Cathedral (1546)

Although on an ancient site of an Anglo-Saxon priory church, the cathedral at Christ Church is one of the smallest cathedrals in the UK, and is only 160ft (49m) long. It was rebuilt several times from the twelfth century onwards and has one of the best collections of seventeenth and eighteenth century stained and painted glass in any English ecclesiastical building.

Other features include the perpendicular roof of the choir with elaborate stone vaulting, St Frideswide's shrine base, Robert Burton's monument and the organ case.

***Christ Church (1546)

'The House', as the college is known is bigger, better and richer than any other college in Oxford. It has tremendous personality in its buildings and its people.

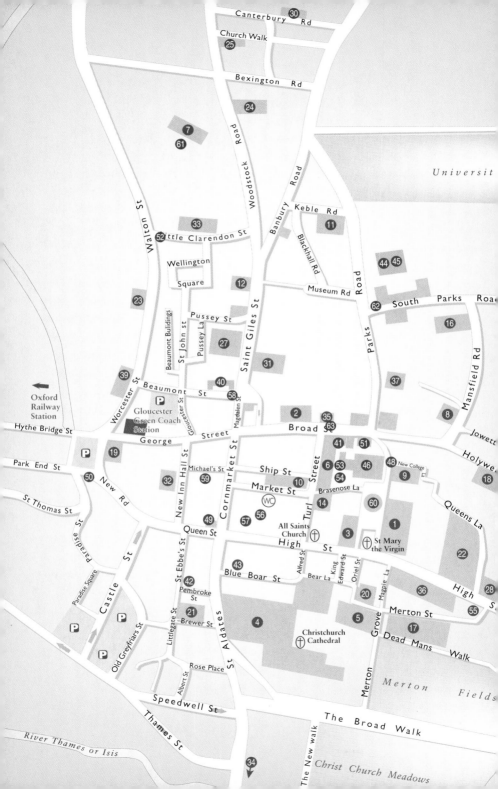

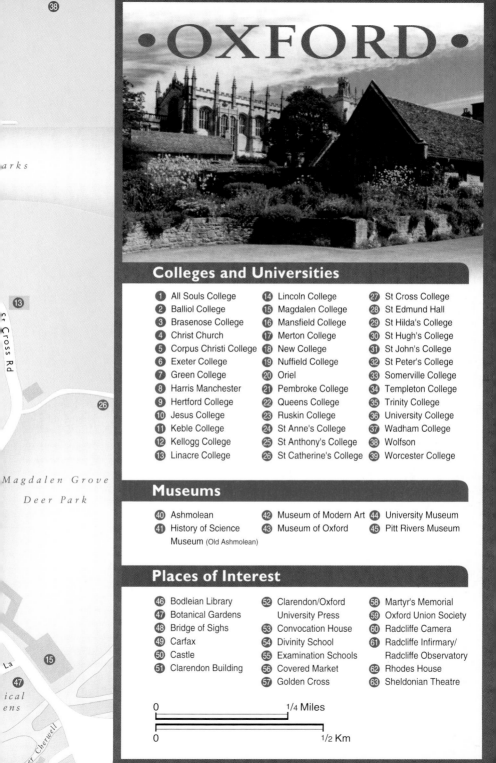

• OXFORD •

Colleges and Universities

1. All Souls College
2. Balliol College
3. Brasenose College
4. Christ Church
5. Corpus Christi College
6. Exeter College
7. Green College
8. Harris Manchester
9. Hertford College
10. Jesus College
11. Keble College
12. Kellogg College
13. Linacre College
14. Lincoln College
15. Magdalen College
16. Mansfield College
17. Merton College
18. New College
19. Nuffield College
20. Oriel
21. Pembroke College
22. Queens College
23. Ruskin College
24. St Anne's College
25. St Anthony's College
26. St Catherine's College
27. St Cross College
28. St Edmund Hall
29. St Hilda's College
30. St Hugh's College
31. St John's College
32. St Peter's College
33. Somerville College
34. Templeton College
35. Trinity College
36. University College
37. Wadham College
38. Wolfson
39. Worcester College

Museums

40. Ashmolean
41. History of Science Museum (Old Ashmolean)
42. Museum of Modern Art
43. Museum of Oxford
44. University Museum
45. Pitt Rivers Museum

Places of Interest

46. Bodleian Library
47. Botanical Gardens
48. Bridge of Sighs
49. Carfax
50. Castle
51. Clarendon Building
52. Clarendon/Oxford University Press
53. Convocation House
54. Divinity School
55. Examination Schools
56. Covered Market
57. Golden Cross
58. Martyr's Memorial
59. Oxford Union Society
60. Radcliffe Camera
61. Radcliffe Infirmary/ Radcliffe Observatory
62. Rhodes House
63. Sheldonian Theatre

0		1/4 Miles
0		1/2 Km

arks

Magdalen Grove

Deer Park

ical ens

St Cross Rd

La

River Cherwell

Interior of Cathedral at Christ Church showing the trefoil, the three arches in ascending order.

Clarendon Building (1711 1724)

A Thomas Hawksmoor building with statues of the Muses by Sir James Thornhill. Sir James also painted the great hall at Blenheim and the altar pieces at All Souls and Queen's College chapels.

Clarendon or Oxford University Press (1830)

A handsome series of buildings in Walton Street designed by Daniel Robinson who also carried out work at All Souls and Oriel colleges.

College Barges

Found along the Isis together with boathouses relics of Georgian times and are floating changing rooms.

Congregation House (1320-30)

Part of St Mary the Virgin.

Convocation House (1634-7)

Part of the Bodleian Library complex which served for both the University's 'parliament' and the Nation's Parliament during the Civil War.

Corpus Christi College (1517)

(See entry, Walking Tour).

*Covered Market (1773-4)

The architect of Magdalen Bridge, John Gwynn, designed a new market to ease the congestion of market stalls that spilled out on streets from Carfax. A collection of interesting shops from fishmongers, game butchers, cheesemongers to shoes (including repairs), flowers, books, jewellery, locksmiths and cafés are to be found. The atmosphere is colourful and lively. Many visitors prefer the covered market to the High Street shops.

Once a year, two clerks of the market are sworn in at the first meeting of Congregation in the Michaelmas Term, an office for which they are paid £5 and are invited to the annual corn-rent dinner by Estate Bursars. There they announce the current price of corn; a relic of the control once exercised by the Gown over the Town.

Cowley

Once a village it is now a suburb created mostly by the motor industry. A building worth seeing is the chapel (1906) of All Saints Convent, St Mary

Road, designed by Sir Ninian Comper. It was the inspiration for Temple Moore's Chapel at Pusey House and with that ranks as the best twentieth-century Gothic in Oxford.

***Divinity School (1430-83)

Part of the Bodleian complex that was even hailed in 1603 by Sir Roger Wilbraham as 'the chiefest wonder in Oxford'.

Examination Schools (1882)

A large striking building, which was inspired by the Elizabethan style of Kirby Hall, Northamptonshire, it launched the prolific career of Sir Thomas Jackson in Oxford. His eclectic work was dubbed Anglo-Jackson as it was composed of elements from English, Italian and Flemish architecture. Such a style he intimated was 'eminently suitable to modern usage, more elastic than Gothic or free classic'. Features include a porch with an arch in the form of a Venetian window at the entrance, a carved panel over the portico, of an undergraduate being hit over the head by a book, a courtyard that faces east onto the narrow Merton Street to ensure a quiet atmosphere for the examinees and the use of the durable Clipsham Limestone on the facade.

Jackson also designed the Ruskin School of Drawing (1886-8) next door and the elegant cricket pavilion in the University Parks. Other buildings include the University's Social Studies Faculty Centre in George Street and the Department of Materials in Banbury Road (southern end), which is different as it is not derived from Elizabethan and Jacobean sources.

Exeter College (1314)

The best building is the magnificent hall with its fine collar-beam roof of Spanish Chestnut, and the rich Jacobean Screen has the coat of arms of Sir John Acland who built it. The chapel has a tapestry of the *Adoration of the Magi* by Burne Jones and William Morris.

Golden Cross

A picturesque courtyard in Cornmarket which was the site of the Crown Inn, owned by Sir William Davenant's father who was also the mayor of Oxford. Shakespeare stayed as their guest on his trips to and from London to Stratford, and it is claimed that he had an affair with Mrs Davenant, a beautiful woman. The room which he occupied on these visits is at No 3 Carfax on the second floor and is known as the Painted Room because of the sixteenth-century designs on the plastered walls.

The Martyr Bishops Ridley and Latimer slept at the Inn in 1555 and Archbishop Cranmer in 1556.

Green College (1979)

Endowed by Dr and Mrs Cecil Green, it has two notable features. The Radcliffe Observatory (1794) first designed by Henry Keene and later by James Wyatt, is architecturally one of the finest of its kind in Europe and the tower was inspired by the Tower of the Winds in Athens. There is also the garden designed by Michael Pirie who creates visual harmony through the imaginative use of plants. One of the best places to see the garden, is from the first floor of the Radcliffe Observatory. Pirie's summer courses at Kellogg College, which are open to the public, are very popular.

Above: Barges along the towpath of the canal

Right : The Cricket pavilion, University Park

Below: The Bridge of Sighs at Hertford College

Opposite page: Interior of the Divinity School, part of the Bodleian Library complex

Harris Manchester (1889)

A splendid set of stained glass windows by Burne Jones in the chapel.

Hertford College (1740)

Although the college started as Hart Hall in 1282, it was refounded in 1824 and most of the new buildings were designed by Sir Thomas Jackson at the end of the nineteenth and beginning of the twentieth century. One interesting feature is the stair tower based on the French Renaissance Chateau at Blois.

Holy Trinity Church (1848-9)

Trinity Road, Headington. Early work of Sir George Gilbert Scott, who also designed Martyr's memorial, and good example of Victorian architecture. Stained glass window by Sir Ninian Comper.

***Iffley Church (1170-80)

An impressive Romanseque building which is one of the best preserved twelfth-century village churches in the Britain. Superb deeply recessed and geometrically patterned arches and windows.

Indian Institute (1883-6)

A yellow building by Basil Champneys, in a free eclectic style, English Renaissance with Oriental details, that resembles that of his rival Sir Thomas Jackson. The institute was founded for 'The work of fostering and facilitating Indian studies in this University; the work of making Englishmen, and even Indians themselves, appreciate better than they have done before the languages, literature and industries of India'.

Jesus College (1571)

Another college in which the founder, Dr Hugh Price, was the son of a butcher. The first two quadrangles of this small college are attractive, particularly the second with its seventeenth-century uniform design, gablets and doorways with four-centred arches. The hall, which was remodelled with wood panelling, has

a Van Dyck portrait of Charles I, and one of Elizabeth I with a wild strawberry, by an unknown artist.

Keble College (1870)

(See entry, Heads of College).

Kellogg College (1990)

The former Rewley House which is now the University's Department for continuing education. It is a set of brick buildings in Wellington Square, the largest surviving residential square.

Lady Margaret Hall (1878)

The college was named after Henry VII's mother, Lady Margaret Beaufort, who had also founded Christ's and St John's colleges at Cambridge. It is in North Oxford on the banks of the Cherwell. Architects were Basil Champneys, and Sir Reginald Blomfield whose French Renaissance style was suited to the use of brick in the buildings. Sir Giles Gilbert Scott's most satisfactory designs in Oxford are found here including the Byzantine – Romanesque chapel in which a feature is the beautiful triptych by Burne Jones.

Linacre College (1962)

Named after Renaissance scholar and physician Thomas Linacre, Fellow of All Souls (1484) and friend of Erasmus.

*Lincoln College (1427)

Established by Richard Fleming, Bishop of Lincoln, it has preserved a fifteenth-century character more than any other college. The chapel (1629–31) is the most splendid of its period in Oxford, particularly the woodwork, the huge classic screen and the stained glass windows, of

which the one in the east depicting Jonah and the Whale is the best.

**Magdalen College (1458)

(See entry, Walking Tour)

Mansfield (1886)

It is the most successful work of Basil Champneys who designed all the buildings in his Gothic style. The library is outstanding due to the ingenious timberwork and steep roof adorned with stylized floral paintings.

Martyr's Memorial (1841-3)

It is a copy of the Waltham Eleanor Cross and was designed by Sir George Gilbert Scott with sculpted figures of Bishops Cranmer, Latimer and Ridley by Henry Weekes. On the orders of Mary I, the Bishops were burnt at the stake.

Merton College (1264)

A series of higgledy piggledy ancient buildings because when it was founded there was no model of an Oxford college to go on. Two buildings worth seeing are the library and the chapel. Victorian architects involved in the remodelling were Basil Champneys (St Albans Quad) and Sir George Gilbert Scott (Hall).

Mesopotamia

Name given to a walk along the Cherwell between the Parks and St Clements that emerges by the Magdalen cricket ground in Marston Road.

Music Room (1742-8)

In Holywell Street. One of the first purpose-built buildings for music performances. It resembles a congregational church and was designed by Dr Thomas Camplin of St Edmund Hall. Handel's *Oratorio* was performed at its opening and during the 1920's Thomas Driberg gave a Dadaist recital of his poetry using a megaphone to the accompaniment of working typewriters and climaxed with loud flushing of a lavatory which is situated in the building.

*New College (1379)

The founder William of Wykeham, Bishop of Winchester and Lord Chancellor, was fortunate to find a large site for his college, officially called St Mary College of Winchester in Oxford, to carry out his concept of collegiate architecture that was a model for all others that followed. He grouped the principal buildings around the quadrangle, the first in Oxford and arranged them in a manner to give the quad a sunny aspect. The kitchen, buttery, larders, servants' and cooks' quarters were out of sight as was the Long Room, which contained the latrines.

Other innovations were to recruit Fellows exclusively from Winchester, to place the Warden's lodgings above the entrance so he could keep an eye on the teenage students and to introduce a T-shaped plan in the chapel. Of note are the Sir Joshua Reynolds' west window, Sir Jacob Epstein's Lazarus, the founder's silver gilt pastoral staff and the wall of sculptures in place of the east window. The incomparable cloisters are to the west with a bell tower (1396-7) and the old city wall. The work of Basil Champneys and Sir George Gilbert Scott are also found at the college.

New Inn Hall Street (formerly Lane of Seven Deadly Sinners)

Frewen Hall (1435) which is now part of Brasenose College, was originally a building for Augustinian Canons. Opposite side is the Wesley Memo-rial Methodist Church (see entry History) whose steeple dominates the street and St Peter's College (1929), whose Chapel, the Church of St Peter-Le-Bailey was designed by Basil Champneys.

Nuffield College (1958)

Founded by Lord Nuffield who started Morris Motors, it was designed by Harrison, Barnes and Hubbard according to his specification of Cotswold domestic architecture. The tower, which is a distinctive element in the Oxford skyline, houses books rather than bells.

**Old Ashmolean (1683)

A fine example of English Renaissance, with outstanding carvings over the doorway by an unknown architect. The building, now the Museum of the History of Science, had a dual purpose, with scientific teaching on the lower floors and a museum above.

Oriel (1326)

(See entry, Walking Tour).

*Oxford Union Society (1857)

The oldest and grandest undergraduate club whose principal features are the debating-hall and library of over 50,000 books. Benjamin Woodward of Dublin designed the Gothic Revival, quirky, octagonal hall with rose windows, the gallery of which was decorated by the Pre-Raphaelites – Rossetti, Burne-Jones and Morris. When the new hall was built by Alfred Waterhouse in 1878, the library moved into Woodward's building.

Park

University Park or 'Parks', is full of sporting activities, including croquet

lawns and suitable for walks as it runs down to the River Cherwell, where there is a famous nude bathing spot called Parson's Pleasure. It also has a cricket pavilion.

Pembroke College (1624)

(See entry Walking Tour).

Port Meadow

Attractive area covering about two miles for rambling or walking along the Isis. There is a boatyard, wild ponies and two pubs, including The Trout located near the end, at Godstow bridge. Common land owned by people of Oxford since Doomsday (1086) when William The Conqueror ordered everything to be recorded. Reached off Walton Street, down Walton Well Road.

Pusey House (1884)

St Giles. Designed by Temple Moore.

**Queens College (1341)

Nicholas Hawksmoor, Sir Christopher Wren and Grinling Gibbons are featured.

***Radcliffe Camera

Part of the Bodleian complex.

Radcliffe Infirmary (1770)

Designed by Henry Keene.

*Radcliffe Observatory (1794)

An original and elegant building.

Rhodes House (1929)

A combination of Cotswold Manor and Old Colonial, it was designed by Sir Herbert Baker to commemorate Cecil John Rhodes. It is a centre for Rhodes scholars with a library containing books on American and Commonwealth history, including works published in these fields since 1760.

Ruskin College (1899)

Founded to provide working men with a chance to study. Today it offers further education for the disadvantaged and excluded.

***Sheldonian Theatre (1669)

One of the most splendid buildings in the Bodleian complex which is open to the public as it is also a venue for concerts.

St Aloysius (1875)

Yellow brick, Roman Catholic Church on Woodstock Road, was designed by Joseph Hansom, an accomplished architect and inventor of the hansom cab, a two-wheeled, horse-drawn cab for two people. The poet, Gerard Manley Hopkins was a priest at the church.

St Anne's College (1878)

One of the larger colleges in the university with some buildings by Sir Giles Gilbert Scott.

St Anthony's College (1950)

Founded by Antonin Besse, a French entrepreneur. It has one of the most

Above left: Brasenose College from the High. The main entrance is in St. Mary's Lane around the corner. Above right: A view of the Radcliffe Camera, the first round library designed by James Gibbs. Below: Interior of the University Museum demonstrating the forest of cast-iron ribs and the dinosaur collection successful contemporary buildings in the colleges, designed by Howell, Killick, Partridge and Amis. The hall and common rooms, which from the outside look like an ominous concrete box, have a pleasant interior.

St Barnabas (1869)

A successful example of Sir Arthur Blomfield's work and one of the best Victorian churches in Oxford.

**St Catherine's College (1963)

A unique college as all the principal buildings were designed by the Danish architect, Arne Jacobsen, who in Bauhaus-style was also responsible for furniture, cutlery and the famous high-backed chairs for the High Table. Here is a splendid example of secular collegiate architecture, which is described as perfect by Nikolaus Pevsner, and by an acerbic wit, as the best motel in Oxford.

St Cross College (1965)

The chapel has Burne-Jones windows.

St Edmund Hall (1278)

Teddy Hall is the only surviving medieval hall of which parts of the ancient quadrangle remain. The library is housed in one of the most interesting churches in Oxford, St Peter-in-the-East, because of its origins in several medieval periods, including the Anglo-Saxon. The vaulted Norman crypt with cushion capitals is believed to be where St Edmund of Abingdon worshipped.

St Hilda's College (1893)

Basil Champneys and Sir Reginald Blomfield, two exponents of brick buildings for female-only colleges are in evidence. The Jacqueline du Pré Concert Hall is an interesting example of modernist architecture by Van Heynigen and Haward.

St Hugh's College (1886)

Two interesting buildings, the Wolfson and Kenyon are contemporary 1960's by David Roberts.

*St John's College (1555)

On St Giles or the Giler, it is the only college still behind a screen of ancient elms. The ghost of Bishop Laud, Charles I's Archbishop of Canterbury, walks headless down the library. The first quadrangle is older than the college as the site was formerly St Bernard's college for Cistercians, a strict Benedictine order. A notable feature is Canterbury quadrangle, the most impressive piece of seventeenth-century architecture with Tuscan colonnades, and the archways at either end are adorned with fan vaults surrounded by bronze statues of Charles I and Queen Henrietta Maria by Hubert Lesueur. The library (1596–8) on the south side, was built from 1,000 loads of stone and timber taken from the former Beaumont Palace in Beaumont Street.

Behind a tiny gate in the middle of the quad lie extensive and fine college gardens, which were planned by both Capability Brown and Humphrey Repton.

St Paul's Church (1835)

Walton Street. A Greek revival church with Ionic columns designed by H J Underwood and now Freud's Café.

St Peter's College (1929)

(See entry, New Inn, Hall Street)

Somerville College (1879)

Buildings by Sir Thomas Jackson and Basil Champneys.

Templeton College (1984)

Buildings by Powell and Moya.

***The High

(See entry, Walking Tour)

*Trinity College (1554-5)

The core of the former college is the site of the Benedictines' Durham College, founded in 1286, of which the small and beautiful fifteenth-century library remains. The chapel is a splendid example of seventeenth-century architecture and the plaster-work and woodwork are excellent with possible Grinling Gibbon touches. Anglo-Jackson buildings by Sir Thomas Jackson stand round the entrance quadrangle and the garden has a lime walk, large seventeenth-century gates and early Sir Christopher Wren buildings.

University College (1249)

(See entry, Walking Tour)

***University Museum (1860)

The best work of Benjamin Woodword in Oxford, which was approved by John Ruskin as it was the only building in Britain that had been built according to principles enunciated in the Seven Lamps and the Stones of Venice. The interior is remarkable in its use of glass and iron, from the forest of cast-iron ribs and columns to the steep glass roof at the centre. It is Gothic art's successful treatment of railway materials and in homage to Ruskin, Gothic colonnades resemble a courtyard of medieval Italian Palazzo.

Wadham College (1610)

Of interest is a classical frontispiece of Sir Nicholas Wadham and his wife over the entrance to the Hall which has original hammerbeam roof.

Wolfson (1966)

Another college like St Catherine's where all principal buildings were designed by the same architect. In this case, Powell and Moya who also built Templeton College.

Worcester College (1714)

Built from original designs by Dr George Clarke. The college entrance is not on the street but consists of quadrangle open to the town. When Clarke died, Henry Keene completed his work as well as building a classical block of rooms overlooking the sunken quadrangle. It is the third of the existing colleges (the others are Trinity and St Johns) with roots to monastic foundations and the row of houses on the south side are evidence of the Benedictines' Gloucester College. Notable amongst its features are the lake contrived out of a swamp, the chapel and the gardens laid out in a fashionable landscape manner by Rev. Richard Greswell.

3 Gown

HEADS OF COLLEGE

To become a head of an Oxford college is a great honour for it is based on merit and the consensus of one's peers. The Master, as heads of Merton, Balliol and University were first called in the thirteenth century, is elected by fellows who give the successful candidate all the responsibility but no power. The use of diplomatic skills is essential as they cannot afford to have one disgruntled fellow who can upset the apple cart. In the past, at least, they lived like royals with a personal staff of maids and butlers. Now like everyone else, they have to deal with the washing-up. The office-bearers, whether they be titled warden, principal, president, provost or rector remain until retiring age, except the Dean at Christ Church who is appointed by the Crown for life. When he dies, Tom tolls a 100 times, one less than normal.

CHRIST CHURCH

Christ Church is the largest and one of the most magnificent of the colleges. It was founded in 1546 by Cardinal Thomas Wolsey whose statue is over the great gate and red cap is displayed in the library. One of the requirements of the statutes is that a clergyman be at its head.

It is not strictly a college because it is also a house of worship or the House of Christ and is known colloquially as the House.

What emerged was that it was a theoretically impossible institution. It has two faces. The college with quadrangles, chapel and other buildings, with alternations of term and vacation, its closing time at 9pm and its 400 or so undergraduates, co-exists as a cathedral establishment of the diocese. This includes all the rights of the Bishop, Dean, Canons and Diocese, which have access and make use of the cathedral. Therefore, it is the only college open 365 days of the year. The two bodies are different in aim and dissimilar in fact. The problem is not solved by logic but by ambulation. The Dean walks up the nave of the Cathedral twice a day at service time as the administrator of the cathedral and at the same time is the head of the House.

Everything works smoothly as the Cathedral is the college chapel and services are sometimes collegiate and diocesan. When the head of House closes Tom Gate, named after Thomas Wolsey, at 9.05pm, the Dean sees to it that the legitimate claims of the Diocese are not precluded. Most of the canons are professors in the university and form part of the governing body.

There is an increasing role for women in the college despite the tradition of discrimination against them. The tutors are always available to the undergraduates the individual attention resulting in very low drop out rates.

One cannot deny the magnificence of the buildings when you

Unique time zone

Another strange fact about the House is that its inhabitants live in another time zone from the rest of the UK. When the great bell or Great Tom in Tom Tower *(left)*, rings its 101 strokes, one for each member of the original foundation, it is five minutes later than anyone else. The students, as the Fellows are called, opted to remain at five minutes west of Greenwich Mean Time when the railway network necessitated uniform time throughout the country. They considered that the newfangled nonsense of railways would never take off.

stand at the centre of Tom Quad, nor the feeling of inspiration to great things. I am sure that many graduates who have cast a last look at the House before they go out into the world have thought that nothing is impossible to achieve. After all, the talents of thirteen prime ministers have been nurtured there and it has produced an author, Lewis Carroll, who created a famous book that rivals the real world of Christ Church.

• CRACKING THE CODE OF ALICE IN WONDERLAND •

Fred Wharton is the Head Custodian at Christ Church and a former member of the police Criminal Investigation Department (CID). As a hobby he has looked for clues in the House to find out the origins of characters and situations in Lewis Carroll's book.

1. The brass firedogs in the fireplaces in Hall would have inspired Alice's elongated neck.
2. Cheshire Cat. Lewis Carroll would look out of the top floor of the library and see the Liddell's cat Dinah lying on a branch of the huge chestnut tree in the garden.
3. White Rabbit. The animal is modelled on Alice's father who also never answered her questions. He is always late as he is running to Christ Church time, which is five minutes later than Greenwich Mean Time. Another similarity is his disappearance down the rabbit hole. When the meal was finished at High Table, her father disappeared behind a secret door that led to the Quad.
4. The Treacle Well. The word has nothing to do with the sticky dark syrup and is derived from the Anglo-Saxon word for cure. The water from the well in Binsey was used by St Frideswide to effect cures to illnesses.
5. The Gryphon and the Mock Turtle. In 1863, the Prince of Wales introduced his bride to the University and was given a banquet at Christ Church at which mock turtle soup was served in two huge turtle shells that hang on the kitchen walls. There is also the Wolsey coat of arms on the walls, which is supported by two Griffins posed in the same way as Wilfrid Dodgson's drawings of these animals. The turtle shells and the coat of arms are the origin of the two animals.
6. Dodo. Dodgson identified himself with the Dodo partly because of his stammer 'Do-do-Dodgson'. He took Alice and her sisters on visits to the University Museum where there is an exhibit of a Dodo.
7. Lion in the Looking Glass. To get the children in the right mood for photographs, Dodgson would take them into Tom Tower and sometimes stroke the bell with a stick. This produced strange tones and gave rise to the Lion's speech that sounded like 'the tolling of a great bell'. But it caused concern amongst academics at the college who complained about odd sounds coming from the Tom Tower. A clock committee was set-up and permission was given to visitors to strike the bell with a special stick covered in felt and for the privilege there was a payment of 2p.

While I was in the Deanery, I noticed a couple of Alice touches. One was the grey and black cat asleep on the armchair, no doubt a descendent of the Cheshire who was based on Dean Liddell's real cat called Dinah. Another was the hidden door in the shape of a false bookcase that was suddenly pushed open by the Head of Christ Church College.

KEBLE COLLEGE

The college was much maligned in the past for its architecture. John Ruskin, who in spite of encouraging the merits of Venetian Gothic in England, would avert his outraged glance each time he passed the building.

However, fashions change and thirty years later, Keble is described in a twenty-first-century architectural guide as 'the most startling, yet also one of the most impressive buildings of the Gothic Revival … The brickwork … was handled in a dazzling display of polychromy…'

The founders were tractarians, members of the Oxford movement which had caused an upheaval with their ideas to restore Catholic teachings and ceremonial within the Anglican Church. The new institution was established in 1870 as a memorial to one of the members, John Keble, who is the only person to have an Oxford College named after him who was neither a benefactor nor saint.

Another distinction is that the first warden, Edward Stuart Talbot, was one of the youngest heads, at 26, who was not even a clergyman – a requirement of the statutes – and he had the gall to tell the founders that he intended to get married. They had preferred a celibate warden.

The original buildings in my opinion, give a strong personality. The Hall is the largest in Oxford and in keeping with the aim of 'gentlemen wishing to live economically', they were accommodated in small rooms situated along corridors rather than large rooms or 'sets' arranged on staircases. All meals would be taken in Hall unlike other colleges where private entertaining in the undergraduates' rooms was a main feature of social life.

There was too a connection with Christ Church as two of the founders, Edward Bouverie Pusey and Henry Parry Liddon were Canons at the House and Talbot, who achieved a Double First in Greats and History, was a pupil of the latter. Ever since, there has been a friendly rivalry between the two large colleges.

The dominant building of the college which was the first complete, new one in Oxford since Wadham in 1612, and the only one built out of brick rather than stone, is the Chapel of cathedral proportions, rising 90ft (27m) with bold buttresses and a spiky skyline, it cuts an imposing figure from the Parks. The interior is a blaze of colour like great medieval churches that can be seen in the mosaics, floor tiles, patterning of the walls and in the windows.

CHAPEL TREASURE

An unusual feature of the structure is the side chapel that houses its treasure, Holman Hunt's picture, *The Light of the World*. The architect of Keble, William Butterfield, so disliked the Pre-Raphaelite painting, that he excluded it from the chapel design and another architect had to be commissioned for the small addition. Other contemporaries such as Thomas Carlyle found the work controversial as it depicted on effeminate Christ carrying a lantern because apparently the artist used two women, Christina Rossetti and Lizzie Siddal, as models.

Keble is a good example of how Oxford is adapting to new demands from the outside world. In the early years, there were 150 male undergraduates from the Anglican community and today, there are 600 of both sexes and many of whom are secular.

The college is also adding a new building which will house a multipurpose theatre and other facilities to improve its conference centre. The academic standards are up as 86 per cent of the finalists gained Firsts or Upper Seconds recently.

MAGDALEN COLLEGE

A college with its own deer park, two river walks, a beautiful tower from which a choir sings annually at 6am on May Day and a school, besides the usual accoutrement for scholars of a hall, a library, chapel and cloisters, exists in Oxford. The name which is written Magdalen but pronounced Maudlin, demonstrates the quirkiness of the English language.

By the time, Edward Gibbon, the author of *Decline and Fall of the Roman Empire* studied at the college in the middle of the eighteenth century, the standard of education had sadly deteriorated.

'I spent 14 months at Magdalen college,' he said, 'they proved the 14 months, the most idle and unprofitable of my whole life ... I was admitted to the society of fellows, and fondly expected that some question of literature would be the amusing and instructive topic of their discourse. Their conversation stagnated in a round of college business, Tory politics, personal anecdotes, and private scandal ...'

The founder of Magdalen

The powerful and clever founder, William of Waynflete, Bishop of Winchester and Lord Chancellor of England, was so proud of his new institution that he entertained three kings there, including the notorious Richard III, and provided a lavish endowment of 55 manor houses to make it the wealthiest foundation in the university. He also ensured its future income by allotting rooms for noblemen who would pay for enjoying the privileges, an innovation followed by other colleges. As a distinction they wore specially braided silk gowns with gold tufts to their caps.

EXETER COLLEGE

The college, which was the smallest and poorest of the medieval foundations, was gifted a magnificent Jacobean Hall by Sir John Acland a well-known west-countryman. The interior, one of the most impressive in Oxford, has an open timber roof of Spanish Chestnut, perpendicular traceried windows and is entered through a richly carved screen with classical motifs, crowned with the Acland arms.

Like Magdalen, it was founded by a Bishop and a politician, Walter de Stapledon in 1314, for laymen from Devon and Cornwall to study philosophy. It stands along the Turl off Broad Street, just inside the north city wall of which a gatehouse, Palmer's Tower, remains.

DONS

Thomas Rowlandson, the English painter and caricaturist did a series of drawings of scenes of Oxford Life in the early 1800s that poked fun at the propriety of the dons or tutors. In one, titled *A Varsity Trick – Smuggling In*, a group of undergraduates lean out of a first floor window and pull up an attractive whore sitting on a looped rope. A figure dressed in an academic gown watches the jollity from the shadows. He is about to pounce and spoil their fun.

Rowlandson had found a worthy target for his talent by attacking the hapless, frustrated dons whose college statutes required them to eschew sex and marriage. The university upheld the Roman notion of celibacy and the only way they could marry was to accept the offer of a living, for example, the position of vicar and leave Oxford.

The debate on the rule came to a head in 1877 when the Royal Commission on University Reform considered the issue. The claims of scholarship were a strong element in the case of those who favoured marriage among dons. They argued that nature refuses to be bound by Founders' wills as she vindicates her rights. Consequently, the best men left Oxford to marry, while the less good men – those who had no desire to marry and whom others did not wish to marry, remained.

The opponents of marriage objected that if Fellows of colleges, senior dons, were allowed to marry, they would never leave Oxford. They would be dons for 60 years not six years, which was the tenure of a fellowship. The upshot was that there would be no vacant places for promising young men and the Senior Common Rooms would be filled with damp, elderly squibs rather than bright young sparks.

The reform was introduced and the statutes were amended but some colleges insisted on a don pernocating (without a wife) in college during term. At Brasenose, for example, a don surrendered his fellowship upon marriage and then was freshly elected as a married man. Although the actions appear to be quirkish, they are the result of a democratic system at work, in which all dons can express their opinion.

Dons' parliament

There is the House of Congregation, or parliament of dons, comprising over 3,500 members from the academic, senior research, library, museum and administrative staff and with whom final responsibility for all legislative matters rest. It is one of several medieval structures still in place at the university. At its head is the Chancellor, a position dating from 1214, who presides over all major ceremonies and is appointed for life. As he also held high office in the church and the state, and because of his unavoidable absences from Oxford, a Vice-Chancellor was appointed to represent him. He effectively is the Chief Executive and is elected for seven years.

Another ancient office is that of the two Proctors, appointed annually and whose names have been recorded from 1267 to the present day. They have wide powers of discipline over the students and like the

Tribuni Plebis during Roman times, they represent the general body of Master of Arts or dons, as well as standing for the common rights of that class.

There are two further bodies: the Convocation, which is a large formal assembly of graduates throughout the world and originates from the sixteenth century, and the Hebdomadal Council, a name that derives from the Greek for seven days, which is responsible for academic policy and strategic direction and meets once a week.

Dons, lords and masters of the undergraduates in the colleges are at the centre for the medieval tutorial system which still is an integral part of university education and getting good results. Essentially, the system consists of one- or two-to-one teaching in which an undergraduate attends a tutorial once a week in a don's room and writes an essay for discussion.

Dons are special people with a long tradition of being erudite, witty, mentors, geniuses and strange and original characters. There was GB Grundy of Corpus, who was a hero of all of his own adventure stories. Anxious to prove that, at the battle of Marathon in the summer of 490 BC, heavily armed Greek soldiers could run for a mile before they engaged in fighting (according to Herodotus) he had a suit of armour constructed and went to the site of the battle in August. There he encased himself in it, ran a mile in the heat and was fighting fit at the end. After the exploit, British tourists were not afraid to go to Greece in August.

Another don, RM Dawkins who never took exercise, at the age of sixty set off on a mule for Anatolia to study Greek dialect. When he arrived later at the coast, he discovered that World War I had begun and he was drafted into the intelligence service. Once he and a naval officer landed on an island to enquire whether it was being used to refuel German U-boats. After talking to a peasant for a half hour, his companion asked him what the answer was. 'Shut up,' said Dawkins, 'He is talking a most fascinating dialect. I have never head it before.'

OXFORD ECCENTRICS

A story that also derives from that period concerns HW Garrod of Merton who was handed a white feather – the symbol of a coward – in a London Street by a young woman who remarked, 'I am surprised that you are not fighting to defend civilisation.'

'Madam, I am the civilisation that they are fighting to defend,' he answered smartly. When someone was over-effusive to him before dinner, he would say 'Come and sit next to me on my deaf side.'

Sir Maurice Bowra, that most eccentric of dons was also characterised as a wit. One day he and a distinguished fellow were watching men going into college. 'It is a terrible thing but I don't know who a single one of them is,' said the fellow. 'Worse still,' replied Bowra, 'they have no idea who we are either.'

A former fellow of Worcester, Mr Rhodes, lived a solitary and unsociable life and from time to time made journeys to London, always on foot, to invest his money and receive his dividends. On one occasion, he walked in from London and found his scout, as servants are known, preparing his rooms. 'Never mind,' he said, 'I'll just take a turn round the Parks to take the stiffness out of my legs.'

Professor Roberston was a widower with no family and was taken care of by an old housekeeper. Just before he died, he calmly instructed her how to treat his corpse, to tie up his chin, to lay him out etc.

John Ruskin was drawing birds' wings on a blackboard in a lecture room one day when a military band struck up outside. He gathered up his gown and fell to marching across the room. 'Gentlemen,' he announced to the audience, 'I cannot resist martial music.'

Dr Frowd, a fellow of Corpus, was irritated at the trampling of grass under his window and set a man-trap to catch the offender. Later he heard a scream and rushed down from the second floor to find that he had snared the Professor of Moral Philosophy. By way of penance he condemned himself to attend the Professor's lectures for the rest of term.

Charles Dodgson

The Rev. Charles Lutwidge Dodgson, better known as Lewis Carroll was one of the sights of Oxford. Strangers, mainly women, begged the locals to point him out and were disappointed when they saw the homely figure with the grave repellent face who never wore an overcoat on his constitutional. Some called him a 'grown-up child' because he remained one in frankness, innocence and simplicity. A man of wide intellectual range and lively imagination, he shrank from adult contact and was a genuine lover of children.

UNIVERSITY PUBLIC ORATOR

The first reference to the office of the Public Orator was made in the sixteenth century during a visit by Queen Elizabeth I to the university, but the tradition is still alive today.

When Elizabeth I arrived in Oxford, the public orator welcomed the Queen at North gate in Latin and delivered another speech in Greek at Carfax. She in turn thanked him in Greek and was then escorted to Christ Church. He then participated in disputations for three days in the royal presence and at the end gave a Latin oration in praise of Her Majesty and her victories over Spain and the Pope.

HONORARY DEGREE CEREMONY

Nowadays, the orator is busy on a couple of occasions a year. The ceremony, which is held annually on 20 June, is part of Encaenia, a celebration in memory of benefactors and founders, and requires a procession of dignitaries in full academic dress from the colleges to the Divinity School, where honorands sign their names in the Degree book and then proceed to the Sheldonian.

4

> 'Sweet city with her dreaming spires...'
> Mathew Arnold

'A definition of an educated man,' according to Sir Humphrey Milford, originator of the *Oxford Dictionary of Quotations*, 'is one who spends 10 per cent of his income on books.'

CITY OF BOOKS

Oxford is a city of books. To catch the mood of the bibliophilic city go to Blackwells on Sundays where highbrows peruse new editions over coffee or to Borders, late at night, when middlebrows make their purchases. But be warned, the sheer numbers of books in the Bodleian, over seven million at the last count, presses heavily on everyone; even undergraduates forsake their screens now and then to heft a volume redolent with age.

GROWTH OF THE BODLEIAN

The Bodleian is a library of record, constantly expanding and therefore termed one of 100 per cent retention. It did in the early days indulge in the practice of self-renewal as most other institutions do whereby an old volume is discarded whenever a new book is accepted. As a result, Francis Bacon's newly published, *Advancement of Learning*, hot from the press in 1605, was eliminated as was the Shakespeare *First Folio*, which had been received in 1623 but was later supplanted by the *Third Folio* through the cavalier policy.

Its four hundred years of growth and expansion out of a fifteenth-century room, which is still its ancient heart, into a complex of some 100 different libraries gives a God's eye view of the world to students and scholars from all over the globe.

Within three months of its opening a French academic was working in the library for six hours a day and some 24 scholars from Germany, the Netherlands, Scandinavia and

Switzerland had tapped its resources.

There were four basic suppositions that has served the library very well. The most powerful universities had the largest collection of books and the principal duty of the librarians was to accumulate and catalogue books. The users could be presumed to know what they were doing and to know what they wanted. Finally, the basic shape of information, knowledge and wisdom was the book, a rectangular form stitched down one side.

David Vaisey, Librarian Emeritus, says books 'are the fuel on which universities run.' Singly, they are user-friendly devices for knowledge, objects of quality that last long and all you need is a pair of eyes (or hands for Braille readers) to benefit.

PLEASURE OF TOUCH

Susan Hitch, an English don at Magdalen, agrees with David Vaisey about the practical and pleasurable aspect of books. 'There's nothing nicer than to be able to handle an old book that has smudge marks of other scholars' thumbs on the pages,' she said. 'It's sharing scholarship down the ages.' Her students are expected to read for between six and eight hours a day, a task which is difficult to do on the screen because of the greater eye strain. 'Although, Anglo-Saxon text is online, it is easy to walk 20 yards to the library and see it in a book.'

The physical sensation of holding and looking at books has its price in wear and tear. Michael Turner, who has worked for over 40 years in the Bodleian, has the responsibility for the upkeep of the collection. His duties are threefold. He protects books through boxing them, either by hand or machine, through controlling the environment and safeguarding them from damp conditions and through the use of acid-free board. The third way, conservation, is the most satisfying.

As his resources are limited, he has to undertake an assessment of the urgency of the repairs, particularly among the medieval manuscripts, 50 per cent of which need attention. A criterion is the frequency of use of a particular volume. In the librarian's eyes, very regular use can be defined as once in ten years. 'The most common repair is when the book sags, dropping free from the covers,' he said. 'Gravity kills books. Don't forget, they can be standing on a shelf for several hundred years.'

Other signs of age include rotting leather and broken spines. But books were made to last in the past through the use of vellum or lambskin binding, and bosses or studs to protect the outside and pages sewn onto the spine on the inside.

He emphasises that his task is essential to the scholar who sooner or later will want to see a manuscript, book or journal, to check on the vellum, examine how a miniature was painted and the quality of a photograph.

READER DAMAGE

But there is also damage inflicted by the readers themselves. Bishop de Bury listed in *Philobiblon* some of the abuses encountered in the fourteenth century, principally when an unclean hand approached a beloved volume: someone who eats fruit or cheese over an open book; defacing a book through writing notes in the margin or cutting it away; allowing books to become covered by dust or flinging them aside. But he is careful to stress that whenever defects are noticed in books they should be promptly repaired, since nothing spreads more quickly than a tear.

After its 400 years of existence, David Vaisey is confident of the library's positive role in the decades ahead. He believes that the library will take the electronic revolution in its stride. 'I suspect computers will deviously chew away at libraries from the inside. They'll eat up book budgets and require librarians that are more comfortable with computers than with children and scholars. Libraries will become adept at supplying the public with fast low-quality information. The remit won't be a library without books – it'll be a library without value.'

In the meantime, the books keep accumulating and the Bodleian keeps expanding to accommodate them.

The Sackler library, a spanking new building that houses over 250,000 books on art and the classics, opened in 2001. It has a further growth space of 10 years and the state-of-the-art climate control to protect books in which tempered air is heated, cooled and humidified but not dehumidified.

Readers' oath

But the centuries-old tradition in the spirit of the *Philobiblon* still applies to readers, who when they are admitted, need to take the following oath:
I hereby undertake not to remove from the library, or to mark, deface, or injure in any way, any volume, document, or other object belonging to it or in its custody; not to bring into the library or kindle therein any fire or flame, and not to smoke in the library; and I promise to obey all rules of the library.

ORIGINS OF BLACKWELLS

Although Blackwells bookshop may seem to have been a permanent feature of the Oxford scene dating back several hundred years, it only opened its doors in 1879. The founder, Benjamin Henry Blackwell, was born in Oxford and a booklover. He taught himself Latin in order to read Caesar's *Gallic Wars* in the original and memorized the catalogue of Bernard Quaritch, who developed the most extensive trade in old books in the world.

His son Sir Basil was also an Oxford man – his college was Merton, and under his guidance the bookshop expanded its premises under Trinity college's quadrangle which was named after the then President, Sir Arthur Norrington.

One of the advantages of running a bookshop like Blackwells is that one can publish books too, for their interests extend to medical, school and academic publishing. An unusual book they printed in honour of Sir Basil's 70th birthday in 1959 was the fourteenth-century work of Richard de Bury, *Philobiblon*, a definitive volume on biblomania. A bishop of Durham, he had more books than all other English bishops put together and in the bedrooms of his many residences, there were always so many books around that it was hardly possible to stand or move without treading on them.

'In books, I find the dead as if they were alive,' he said, 'in books, I foresee things to come; in books warlike affairs are set forth, from books come forth the laws of peace … all the glory of the world would be buried in oblivion, unless God had provided mortals with the remedy of books.'

All you need to know about Blackwells

Email: oxford@blackwellsbookshops.co.uk
Blackwell's, 50 Broad Street, Oxford, OX1 3BQ ☎ 01865 792792

The unofficial university bookshop with over five miles of shelving. It is one of the largest in the world that is still family-owned. Also selection of rare books. A coffee shop that offers sandwiches and cakes with views overlooking the Sheldonian Theatre.

The Art and Poster Shop, 27 Broad Street.
☎ 01865 333641

Music Shop, 23-25 Broad Street.
☎ 01865 249600

Children's books, 8 Broad Street.
☎ 01865 333694

Opening Hours – Monday to Saturday 9am–6pm. Tuesday 9.30am–6pm. Sunday 11am–5pm

Walking tours of Oxford, including literary and historic interest.
☎ 01865 333606, or enquire in bookshop.

BOAR'S HILL

There are several vantage points overlooking Oxford and none so attractive as Boar's Hill which is about four miles from the centre and provides a superb view. The name is a misnomer as early charts show the presence of boreholes and the title of Bore's Hill. There is also the legend of the undergraduate who killed a wild boar on the hill in Bagley wood by thrusting a copy of Plato's works down its throat.

It was a sandy, barren tract of fir-planted land with a row of smuggler's cottages down a side called Old Boar's Hill that became a suburb for married dons when North Oxford was considered crowded, stuffy and Victorian.

Hidden golf course

Sir Arthur Evans, archaeologist and discoverer of King Minos' palace at Knossos, Crete was one of the first academics to move there. He built Jarn mound at the top of the hill to commemorate his find. Lord Berkely, another early settler, was keen on science and built a tower with a laboratory and a golf course surrounded by a six-foot wooden fence because he liked to play in private. (His house has been turned into the Open University and the golf course is for public use and provides good tobogganing in winter.)

The heights have always attracted the literary set, poseurs, octogenarians and Maud and Albie Sunday Socials.

A view of Oxford from Boar's Hill.

POETS AND AUTHORS

There were once two Poet Laureates who both lived on the Hill and for kicks sometimes they raced each other down. The younger of the two, **John Masefield**, was so self-effacing that he never submitted an official poem to *The Times* without sending a self-addressed envelope in case they thought it was not good enough to publish.

His predecessor, **Robert Bridges**, was made of sterner stuff and dressed the part in a cloak, with a sombrero on his leonine head of white hair and sported a red bowtie.

He worked in a little summer house in the garden of his home Chilswell House. It was an unusual place as the interior was always bathed in a golden glow through skilful arrangement of subdued lighting and yellow silk hangings. There is an anecdote about his later years when he no longer drove but used a taxi. He would always ask the driver to stop halfway up the Hill where he could see his home. One day, while the taxi waited, he heard Dr Bridges give a mighty sigh of relief. The driver enquired the reason.

'I always had a premonition that my house would catch fire,' he said.

'Well at last its happened. So let's hurry back to put it out.'

Another denizen of the Hill was **Robert Graves** whose wife ran the post office on Fox Lane to make ends meet. Graves later effected the same style of dress as Dr Bridges when he lived on Deya, Majorca. **Mathew Arnold** tramped about Bagley woods on the Hill where he discovered a camp of gypsies and his poem the Gipsy Scholar is commemorated with a plaque in a field. He was also inspired to produce the lines, '... sweet city with her dreaming spires ...'

A Jesuit priest from St Aloysius Church, **Gerard Manley Hopkins**, also sung its praises in his original sprung rhythm, 'Towery city and branchy between towers.'

'cuckoo-echoing, bell swarmed, lark charmed, rook-racked, river-rounded'.

Auden who spent his last years at his alma mater, Christ Church, which had taken him in providing him with a house in the college grounds, was also a visitor on the Hill during his undergraduate days. He wrote the border-country poetry, which marked his transition to adult work, in the long vacation following his second year at Oxford.

Both C S Lewis and J R R Tolkien were admirers of old Icelandic sagas and myths and formed a club, the Coalbiters, where passages would be read and discussed. The name derived from Icelandic or Old Norse, Koltibar, meaning 'men who lounge so close to the fire that they bite the coal'.

'One week I was up till 2.30 on Monday,' wrote Lewis to a friend on 3 December 1929, talking to the Anglo-Saxon Professor Tolkien, who came back with me to college from a society and sat discoursing of the gods and giants of Asgard for three hours, then departing in the wind and rain – who could turn him out, for the fire was bright and the talk good.'

Tolkien was an orphan who lost his father at the age of four and his mother when he was twelve, and found solace in his love for 'Northernness.' In child-hood, he fell under the spell of the fairy story about Sigurd and Völsung who slew the dragon Fafnir and henceforth 'desired dragons with a profound desire.'

He taught himself the Norse language and during adolescence began to write his own Norse poetry and dramas. Lewis had done the same as a teenager but soon passed on to other types of writing and poetry, whereas for Tolkien, Northernness remained the centre of his imaginative endeavours throughout his life. He knew he was on the right track when after his late-night discussion with Lewis, he sent him the Beren and Luthien poem which was part of the *Silmarillon* and received an encouraging letter back.

'Just a line to say that I sat up late last night,' wrote his friend on 7 December 1929, *'and have read the geste as far as where Beren and his gnomish allies defeat the patrol of the orcs above the sources of the Narog and disguise themselves in the reaf. I can quite honestly say that it is ages since I have had an evening of such delight; and the personal interest of reading a friend's work had very little to do with it – I should have enjoyed it just as well if I'd picked it up in a bookshop, by an unknown author.*

'The two things that come out clearly are the sense of reality in the back-ground and the mythical value: the essence of a myth being that it should have no taint of allegory to the maker and yet should suggest incipient allegories to the reader. So much at the first flush. Detailed criticisms (including grumbles at individual lines) will follow.'

The friendship between the two was of profound importance to Tolkien because he gained confidence from Lewis's enthusiasm and realised that his 'stuff' as he called it could be more than just a hobby and indeed he created a whole new mythology, including invented languages. He had married Edith Bratt, who came from a similar childhood and it was a difficult period for him bringing up four children at his home in North Oxford. 'Friendship with Lewis compensates for much,' he wrote in his diary.

Once the coalbiters had read the major Icelandic sagas and both Eddas, the club was disbanded and later a new group, the Inklings, was formed. They met on Tuesdays to drink beer in the Bird and Child (now the Eagle and Child in St Giles) and on Thursdays in Lewis' Magdalen college rooms to read aloud from their works-in-progress.

The group was in reality a launching pad for bestsellers such as *The Hobbit* and the *Lord of the Rings* from Tolkien and Lewis's classic Narnia books for children, among others. How near the nerve his work was to Tolkien is shown in a letter.

'I resemble a Hobbit at any rate in being moderately and cheerfully domesticated, though no cook.'

What is evident about Oxford is its strong influence on children's literature, from the master of the genre, Lewis Carroll, and Tolkien and Lewis to Kenneth Grahame with *Wind in the Willows*. Grahame worked in a bank like T S Eliot and wrote his classic as bedtime stories for his son Alistair. He created unforgettable characters like Toad, and Badger who has to keep his friend always in check.

'The clever men at Oxford know all that is to be knowed, but they none of them know one half as much as intelligent Mr Toad.'

His son Alistair, who was very much in the shadow of his famous father, could not live up to his expectations while an undergraduate at Christ Church and threw himself under a train near Port Meadow. They both share a grave at Holywell cemetery.

LEWIS CARROLL

Lewis Carroll, which was the pseudonym Charles Lutwidge Dodgson first used for articles in train magazines is undoubtedly one of the greatest children's writers in the world.

He was fortunate in the choice of a muse, the seven-year-old Alice Liddell, the daughter of the Dean of Christ Church where he was a mathematics don. She with her 'pure, unclouded brow and dreaming eyes of wonder' was his greatest inspiration. An attractive girl, she was prime motivator in his new hobby

of photography, which was in vogue in the 1850s and a means of advancement in Oxford society. Eligible young ladies and young children were eager to agree to 'sit' before the camera, fascinated by the antics of the photographer beneath his black focussing cloth, and they would become objects of admiration when the results were shown in albums.

The Liddell children, Edith (the eldest), Alice and Ina (the youngest) who lived in the Deanery were ideal subjects because they were close at hand, and Alice, whom he had known since the age of four, was his favourite. Undoubtedly, she appeared to him as a woman-child whom he desired to please and as she liked to be the centre of attraction, she was a central figure in the stories.

'We used to sit on the big sofa on each side of him while he told us stories,' she wrote later in 1932, 'illustrating them by pencil or ink drawings as he went along ... . He seemed to have an endless supply of these fantastical tales.

'When we were thoroughly happy and amused at his stories, he used to pose us, and expose the plates before the right mood had passed. Being photographed was a joy to us and not a penance as it was to other children.'

It was a memorable trip down the river with his fellow Oxford don, Robinson Duckworth, for a picnic that gave rise to the first of the two Alice books.

'Duckworth and I made an expedition up the river to Godstow with the three Liddells,' so wrote the 30-year-old don in his diary, 'we had tea on the bank there, and I did not reach Christ Church again til quarter past eight ... On which occasion, I told them the fairy-tale of Alice's Adventures Under Ground ...'

According to Duckworth, the story was spoken over his shoulder for the benefit of Alice and he was told by Dodgson that it was being invented as he went along. When they returned to the Deanery Alice asked him to write out the adventures for her.

Women at Oxford

'Before 1878, there were no women dons, no women undergraduates, no women's colleges,' wrote Dacre Balsdon, the donnish author of *Then and Now*. 'And there were the untouchables – the womenfolk of the leeches and of attorneys, people to whom the ladies in the lodgings conceded the right to exist, but not the right to exist socially. The untouchables, of course, sometimes had pretty daughters, "toasts", who were marked in the eyes of the prudent undergraduate "for amusement only".'

After 1880, women were admitted to the university and then had to wait another 40 years before being permitted to take degrees and become full members of it.

SIXTEENTH-CENTURY ATTITUDES

Anthony Wood, antiquary and Merton man, recorded in his Annals (1549) the stir caused by allowing wives into Christ Church. He observed that it 'was looked upon as such a damnable matter by the Catholics that they styled them whoores, and the lodgings that entertained married women and children, stews, and conyburies.'

By the late 1890s five women's colleges had been established in Oxford with female principals and tutors. But their marginality was still emphasized as they were spaced around the outskirts of the city, shut out by a cordon of river, parks, North Oxford housing and shopping precincts. They were apart too through their architecture for they were not awe-inspiring and grandiose like the men's colleges, but had pretty gardens and the buildings set a precedent in Oxford, as they provided a protective, domestic environment essential for well-bred young ladies.

Bluestocking

The discomfort of having female academics around them has resulted in a special category being created denoted by the word, bluestocking. The origin of the word is interesting because it hints at not being totally equal. It was defined as a man who wore blue worsted stockings instead of the formal black silk and was extended to mean being in informal dress. Later, the term denoted women who attended literary assemblies and were known as blue-stocking ladies or blue-stockingers.

Excursions Outside Oxford

5

EXCURSIONS OUTSIDE OXFORD

Oxford is an ideal base for touring the Cotswolds, the Chilterns and the Thames Valley. Close to the city is the pretty town of Woodstock with the world heritage site of Blenheim Palace birthplace of Winston Churchill and home of the Duke of Marlborough. There are other grand homes such as **Waddesdon,** home of Lord Rothschild or **Stonor,** of Lord and Lady Camoys, which is in the Chiltern Hills near Henley. Other sights include the moated Elizabethan Manor, **Broughton Castle**, near Banbury and the sixteenth-century **Kelmscott Manor**, the summer home of the artist and craftsman William Morris near Lechlade. **Thame, Dorchester-on-Thames** (a Roman walled town) and **Wallingford** are near and worth visiting. There is also the **White Horse** at Uffington, a huge chalk outline of a horse carved into the hillside, which is considered to date back to 100 BC.

To the west of Oxford lie the famous stone villages of the Cotswolds, including the historic coaching town of **Burford**, which is set in the Windrush Valley and is an antique centre. Other notable towns are **Great**

A river god in the gardens at Blenheim Palace

Tew, **Broadway** and **Stow-on-the-Wold**. To the south-east is **Henley on Thames**, site of the popular summer regatta and **River and Rowing Museum**, and **Marlow**.

BLENHEIM

WINSTON CHURCHILL

Sir Winston Churchill was born at Blenheim Palace and by lucky accident met his future wife there. His mother, Lady Randolph, was seven months pregnant when she slipped while out with a shooting party in the park. A couple of days later labour began in a pony carriage that rode over uneven ground. She was immediately taken back to the palace where a small ground floor bedroom, west of the Great Hall was set aside for her. It was there on 30 November 1874, that Winston was born.

Later he met Clementine Hozier and invited her down to the palace. He had impressed her with his talk when he said 'Most of us are worms but I'm a glow worm.' He was shy and on the third day pushed by his cousin Sunny, the ninth Duke of Marlborough, he decided to propose. They went for a walk and as it began to rain, they sheltered in the ornamental Temple of Diana. There at the lakeside he asked Clementine to marry him and she accepted.

THE PALACE

Blenheim Palace, which featured large in Sir Winston's life was built as a national monument to another great British hero and ancestor of his whom he admired, John Churchill, the First Duke of Marlborough. The Duke was a brilliant soldier and on numerous occasions won victories against the French and their allies. One of his greatest triumphs was over Louis XIV, who was intent on seizing Vienna and was stopped at the battle of Blenheim, a small town in Bavaria where some 30,000 of the enemy were killed. Queen Anne showed her appreciation of his glorious victory on the Danube in 1704 through a grant of the Royal Manor of Woodstock and funds to build a palace.

Blenheim, according to Sir Nikolaus Pevsner, ranks in scale and magnificence with the great Baroque palaces of Europe and as a work of art, surpasses many of them in quality. It was designed by Sir John Vanbrugh who first had success as a dramatist and later as an architect. The Duke met 'Van' at the playhouse, where one of his plays were performed, and impressed by the model of Castle Howard, which he was building, offered him a commission to build the palace.

It took 20 years to complete, during which 'Van' fell from favour and the Duchess who managed the project appointed Hawksmoor to finish the decoration of the library, the chapel, the kitchen court and various outbuildings.

Love story

A story, which should be told, is of the love borne between the Duke and his Duchess Sarah, the daughter of Richard Jennings. During the early days of their marriage when he was on campaigns, she wrote to him. 'Wherever you are, while I have life, my soul shall follow you, my every dear Lord Marl, and wherever I am I should only kill the time wishing for night that I may sleep and hope the next day to hear from you.'

Another letter written, when she was old and alone, to the Duke of Somerset, who had sought her hand is another avowal of love, to a husband who died over two decades before her death. 'If I were young and handsome as I was, instead of old and faded as I am, and you could lay the empire of the world at my feet, you should never share the heart and hand that once belonged to John, Duke of Marlborough.'

Seen from a distance the silhouette of turrets and pinnacles makes it appear as a romantic castle sited near a lake and in a magnificent park. Each of the rooms from the Great Hall, the Green and Red drawing rooms, to the library and saloon are beautifully decorated and furnished, many with original items such as murals, paintings and woodwork. Proceeding through the palace is like entering and experiencing part of living in the eighteenth century. Indeed, the present Duke is proud of the immaculate condition in which the palace and gardens are kept.

The gardens, which are spread over 2,000 acres (810 hectares) of landscaped parkland, has a lake designed by 'Capability' Brown and a variety of visual delights, including water terraces, a ground cascade, Hawksmoor's triumphal arch, a gigantic column of victory, the world's largest hedge maze, and Rosamund's twelfth-century well. The Fair Rosamund was the youngest daughter of Baron de Clifford and lover of King Henry II. The King built her a cottage near his hunting-box, Woodstock Manor. It was over a spring and had a square well in which she bathed. His wife, Queen Eleanor of Acquitaine found out about the affair and had her poisoned.

One of the most popular features of the palace is the room in which Sir Winston was born. Visitors still marvel over his golden curls cut from his head at the age of 5 years old. No expense has been spared for the Churchilliana in the exhibition near the birth room that includes his paintings, letters and even voice recordings of his speeches.

'We can look back now on the pattern of Sir Winston's life,' wrote his cousin Sunny 'and see … a pleasing inevitability. His birth at Blenheim, his proposal of marriage here beside the lake, his burial at Bladon (within view from the south lawn) – these things form a mosaic which seems almost too neat to be true.'

69

BLENHEIM PALACE
A WORLD HERITAGE SITE

HOME OF THE 11TH DUKE OF MARLBOROUGH
BIRTHPLACE OF SIR WINSTON CHURCHILL

- SET IN 2100 ACRES OF GLORIOUS
  CAPABILITY BROWN PARKLAND
- RESTAURANT, CAFES AND SHOPS
- HERB GARDEN, BUTTERFLY HOUSE
  AND MARLBOROUGH MAZE

PALACE OPEN DAILY FROM
MID MARCH TO 31ST OCTOBER
10.30AM-5.30PM (last admission 4.45pm)

01993 811325
www.blenheimpalace.com

Lady Henrietta Spencer Churchill

Lady Henrietta Spencer Churchill, eldest daughter of the 11th Duke of Malborough, spent a happy childhood at Blenheim where she waterskied on the lake, rode in the park and spent hours walking among the unusual ornaments of the palace roofs. From the moment , at the age of twelve, she was allowed to design her own bedroom, set was set on course for life as an interior designer.

The hours spent exploring the endless concealed staircases and different towers and levels of Blenheim, coupled with a lifelong curiosity about other people's houses, have given focus to her artistic talents, inherited from both her parents.

She is an expert on classical interior decoration and an author of several books on interior design. Her business is based in a charming shop, Woodstock Designs in the High Street, not far from Blenheim Palace.

WOODSTOCK DESIGNS
Interior Design

Complete Interior Design Service
Established in 1981

Woodstock Designs offers a professional, friendly and efficient interior design and decoration service to suit all styles, budgets and ages.

We specialise in residential design, from the renovation of old properties to new build in classic styles. We undertake all aspects of building work, as well as soft furnishings, antiques and accessories.

No job is too big or too small and commissions are undertaken worldwide.

Our resources and access to specialist tradesmen is limitless, whether a pair of curtains or a hand carved and gilded console table.

For professional guidance, inspiration and practical solutions contact one of our team of designers or visit our showrooms.

7 High Street, Woodstock
Oxfordshire, OX20 1TE
Tel: 01993 811887
Fax: 01993 813487

26 Sulivan Road
London SW6 3DX
Tel: 020 7731 8399
Fax: 020 7731 8856

Broughton Castle

Broughton, Banbury, Oxfordshire OX15 5EB
2 miles west of Banbury Cross on B405
Fine moated castle, dated from 1300. Family home of Lord and Lady Saye and Sele, the castle has been in the same family for over 600 years. 3 acre moat, Medieval Great Hall, Civil War Armour and armour, location for scenes in Shakespeare in Love.
Opening Times: Open Late May - early September, Wednesday and Sundays and additional days in July and August. Check ahead for opening times. Groups welcome on any day throughout the year by appointment.
Admission
Adults £5, Concessions £4, Children £2
☎ 01295 722 547
e-mail: admin@broughtoncastle.demon.uk

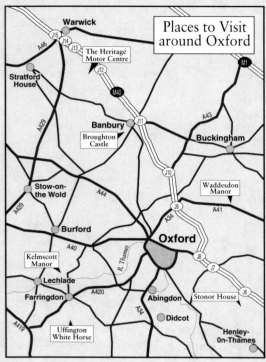

Places to Visit around Oxford

The Heritage Motor Centre

Off Junction 12 M40
Banbury Road, Gaydon, Warwick CV35 0BJ
The largest collection of historic British cars in the world. Over 200 vehicles on display charting the history of the British car industry. Off road demonstration course. Weekends and school holidays: children's quad bikes and electric cars.
Open every day 10.00am - 5.00pm

Admission: Adults £8, Concessions £7, Children (5-16) £6. Under 5's free. Family ticket (2 adults & 3 Children) £25
☎ 01926 641188

Kelmscott Manor

Kelmscott, Lechlade, Gloucestershire G17 3HJ
Grade 1 listed Tudor farmhouse next to the River Thames. Summer home of William Morris.
Opening Times
April-September every Wednesday 11am-1pm & 2pm-5pm
3rd Saturday in April, May, June &

September 2pm-5pm
1st & 3rd Saturday July & August
2pm-5pm
Last entry 30 minutes before closing
Admission: Manor and Gardens
Adults £7, Students and Children
£3.50
Gardens Only Adults £2.00, tudents
and Children Free
Private visits by arrangement
☎ 01367 252486 e-mail:
admin@kelmscottmanor.co.uk

Stonor House

Situated 4.5 miles north of Henley-
on-Thames, off B480
Family home of the Stonor family
for over 800 years. Now the home of
Lord and Lady Camoys.
House features: Tudor exterior,
furnished rooms, paintings, sculptures, belongings of Edward Cam-
pion, gardens, extensive deer park.
Mass celebrated in chapel on
Sundays
Admission: Telephone ahead for
opening times ☎ 01491 638587

Waddesdon Manor

Waddesdon Manor stands on a
hilltop overlooking Aylesbury Vale in
Berkshire, was formerly the family
home of the Rothschilds. The manor
house, modelled on a French
chateau, is also open to the public.
18th century furniture, English
portraits and Dutch Old Masters.The
garden is known for its seasonal
displays, colourful shrubs and
mature trees. Parterre. Aviary.
Opening Times: daily 10am-5pm,
from March - 3rd week in December

Admission: Adults, House and
Grounds £10, Grounds only £3
Children (5-16) House and Grounds
£7.50, Grounds only £1.50
National Trust members Free
Timed tickets to the house can be
bought in adavnce (Advance
booking charge £3 per transaction)
Booking Office ☎ 01296 653226

White Horse

Uffington, Oxfordshire
One and half miles due South of
Uffington, on Berkshire Downs
about 30 mins from Oxford
The White Horse is cut out of turf
on the chalky upper slopes of
Uffington Castle near to the
Ridgeway. It is 374 feet long. The
Uffington White Horse is Britain's
oldest and most famous hill figure.
Parking at Woolstone hill. Short but
steep15 minute walk to horse.
Open all year. Admission free

Timothy Walker, Superintendent of the Botanic Garden is also known by the Latin title, Horti Praefectus as one would expect from a university institution dating back to 1621. He shares the day-to-day management with the Horti Custos or keeper, the Sheradian Professor of Botany.

He stressed the education and research aspect of the garden as it fulfils an integral role in teaching of undergraduates in the biological sciences. In recent years it again has become involved in the training of medical students who are required to understand alternative forms of treatment derived from plants.

He recommends that keen gardeners should also include excursions to five other sites while in Oxford.

Harcourt Arboretum at Nuneham Courtney

This is also run by the University of Oxford. It is situated on a locally rare deposit of greensand and the acid soil enables cultivation of many species intolerant of the soil conditions in Oxford. Filled with the oldest and tallest redwoods in Oxfordshire, there are azaleas and rhododendrons in May and June and the Japanese maples in October. Open: Daily 10am–5pm, May–October. Monday–Friday 10am–4.30pm, November–April.

Rousham Park House and Garden near Steeple Aston

Open all year round and 'is the place to die for,' according to Tim Walker. 'It is big and enchanting,' he said 'and better than Blenheim.' The house and the formal garden has been in the hands of the same family, the Dormers, for the past 300 years. The garden was designed by William Kent who composed landscape as a painter would and is one of the few of this period that escaped alter-ation. The gardens at Rousham are all curves and are a reaction to geometric layout in an attempt to make a naturalistic landscape. 'Rousham is uncommercial and unspoilt with no tea room and no shop,' said a family spokesman. 'Bring a picnic, wear comfortable shoes and it is yours for the day.' ☎ 01869 347110 or 0860 360407 Note: Parties by arrangement. No children under 15 or dogs.

Brook Cottage, Alkerton

This is a four-acre hillside garden of recent origin, which was first established almost 40 years ago. There are a wide variety of trees, over 200 shrubs, a water garden, alpine scree, many clematis and it is interesting throughout the season. ☎ 01295 670303/590. Can be combined with a visit to Broughton Castle. Open: Monday–Friday 9–6, 16 April to 31 October.

Broughton Castle

(see places to visit around Oxford page 72)

Waddesdon Manor

(see places to visit around Oxford page 73)

ACCOMMODATION

Oxford is a popular destination and all kinds of accommodation is available from luxury hotels to a youth hostel.

Luxury

Old Bank Hotel
92-94 High Street
Oxford
OX1 4BN
☎ 01865 799599
Fax: 01865 799598
E-mail: info@oldbank-hotel.co.uk
43 bedrooms, including suites.
A designer hotel in the heart of the city, situated on one of the world's great streets. The hotel building dates back to Elizabethan times and the interior,which was designed by the Parisian, Gladys Wagner,is understated classic elegance. Each bedroom has an individual colour theme in luxurious fabrics that create the impression of a home and most have good views, particularly room 45. Two bonuses of the hotel are The Quod restaurant and bar, where local café society gather, and parking space which is at a premium in the centre. The service is friendly and businessmen will feel at home too because of facilities offered. Cultural visitors can start their Oxford tour at the hotel for it has a permanent exhibition of twentieth century art and a collection of superb photographs.

Old Parsonage Hotel
1 Banbury Road
Oxford
OX2 6NN
☎ 01865 310210
Fax: 01865 311262
E-mail: info@oldparsonage-hotel.co.uk

30 bedrooms including suites
A hotel that resembles a manor house in the country and yet is in the centre of the city. Located in a building which is as old as the colleges, but has all the accoutrement of a luxury hotel that puts guests in great comfort and ease. The rooms have the charm of English country homes and have been restored to their original seventeenth-century design with views over the secluded walled garden. In summer meals can be taken on the front terrace. A good cuisine is offered in the bar area which is an ideal place for an intimate rendezvous. Excels in personal attention.

Randolph Hotel
Beaumont Street
Oxford
OX1 2LN
☎ 0870 400 8200
Fax: 01865 792133
E-mail: randolph@acdonald-hotels.co.uk
119 rooms, including suites
This mammoth Gothic hotel built in 1866 is a well known city landmark opposite the Martyrs' Memorial and the Ashmolean Museum. Most people mistake this premier hotel as having connections with Lord Randolph Churchill, but it was named after an academic with the same surname. It is what guests would expect from a luxury establishment amidst the hustle and bustle of a city centre with its two well appointed restaurants, two lounges and a

bar together with extensive conference facilities. The rooms are lavishly furnished in keeping with its long established reputation as a top hotel.

Moderate

Four Pillars Hotel
Abingdon Road
Oxford
OX1 4PS
☎ 01865 324324
Fax: 01865 324325
E-mail: enquiries@four-pillars.co.uk
115 rooms, including suites
A new quality hotel that belongs to a small group, it is similar to an Oxford college as it enables a guest to be in a closeted environment surrounded by parkland and yet within easy reach of the centre and famous places like Christ Church. The rooms are quiet and furnished in English country style and there are adequate leisure facilities like a swimming pool and gym. A sister hotel, situated four miles from the centre at Sandford on Thames incorporates medieval buildings, a riverside setting, a launch that takes guests into Oxford and a nineteenth-century barge.

Inexpensive

Holiday Inn
Peartree Roundabout
Woodstock Road
Oxford
OX2 8JD
☎ 0870 400 9086 Fax: 01865 553245
An international brand which is conveniently situated on the ring road round Oxford.

Hostels

YHA (Youth Hostel Association)
2a Botley Road
Oxford
OX2 OAB
☎ 01865 727275 Fax: 01865 251182
E-mail: oxford@yha.org.uk
41 rooms
The new building is centrally located, conveniently next to the station and offers accommodation to a wide range of guests from tourists and students to families.

The Tourist Information Centre
can assist in booking rooms in hotels, guest houses, inns and bed and breakfasts (B&B's).

15-16 Broad Street
Oxford
OX1 3AS
☎ 01865 726871 Fax: 01865 240261
Open: Monday–Saturday, 9.30am–5pm. Sunday 10am–3.30pm.

ART GALLERIES AND MUSEUMS

*Ashmolean
Beaumont Street
☎ 01865 278015/278000
Open Tuesday–Saturday, 10am–
5pm. Sunday 2pm–5pm.
Wednesday 10am–8pm May–
July.
Housed in a nineteenth-century
building, it is a museum and an
art gallery, and named after a
seventeenth-century collector
Elias Ashmole. In both instances,
the collections are one of the
finest in Europe and contain a
little bit of everything. The museum section has eclectic items
such as King Alfred's jewel
dating to the ninth century, Lady
Hamilton's dress, King Henry
VIII's stirrups and Sir Arthur
Evans' (a former keeper) incomparable artefacts from his exca-
vation at Knossos, Crete, where
the legendary King Minos,
Daedalus and Icarus originate.
The art section also includes a
wide selection featuring British
and European paintings from the
Middle Ages to the present,
including Uccello's *Hunt in the
Forest*, Cosimo's *Forest Fire*,
drawings of the Old Masters,
watercolours by Turner and
Ruskin and in the new Sands
Gallery, a landscape by the 19-
year-old Picasso, sculptures of
Maillol, Moore, Epstein and
Frink. There are also displays of
oriental and classical art. An
ideal place to spend a day in
inclement weather as a café is
also attached.

Christ Church Picture Gallery
Canterbury Gate
Oriel Square
Oxford OX1 1DP
☎ 01865 276172
Fax: 01865 202429
Open Monday–Saturday,
10.30am–1pm, 2pm–4.30pm.
Sunday 2pm–4.30pm.
An unusual feature of a college
that has a painting school. A
permanent collection of European Old Masters and their
drawings, mainly fourteenth to
eighteenth-century Italian.

Museum of Modern Art (MOMA)
Pembroke Street
Oxford
OX1 1BP
☎ 01865 722733
Email: info@moma.demon.co.uk
Open: Tuesday–Sunday, 11am–
6pm, Thursday 11am–9pm.
A gallery which pioneers exhibi-
tions of twenty-first century
painting, sculpture, photography,
film, video, architecture, design
and performance. Café attached.

Museum of Oxford
Town Hall
St Aldates
Oxford
OX1 1DZ
☎ 01865 252761
One of the most exciting displays
of all the museums in the city
which gives a fascinating glimpse
of Oxford's history from prehistoric times to the present. Of
note are the reconstructed rooms
in houses from Elizabethan to
Victorian period, Alice Liddell's
memorabilia and a nineteenth-
century circular iron staircase
with small wooden block steps.

***University Museum of Natural History
Parks Road
Oxford
OX1 3PW
☎ 01865 272950/270949
E-mail: info@oum.ox.ac.uk
Website: oum.ox.ac.uk
Open Monday–Saturday, 12–5pm.
One of the best museums in the city for both adults and children. It is crammed full of interesting exhibits in zoology, entomology, geology and mineralogy. Outstanding features are the building interior, the dinosaur collection, including a 40ft Tyrannosaurus rex, the extinct (Alice's) Dodo and the huge live cockroaches in the upper gallery.

Pitt Rivers Museum
(behind the university museum)
Parks Road
Oxford
OX1 3PP
☎ 01865 270927
E-mail: prm@prm.ox.ac.uk
Website: prm.ox.ac.uk

Open Monday–Saturday, 1–4.30pm. Sunday 2–4pm. Interesting exhibits in this dark Aladdin's Cave from the collections of General AH Lane-Fox Pitt-Rivers, including muskets, shrunken heads, mummies and a three-floors-high totem pole.

***Museum of History of Science
Old Ashmolean Building
Broad Street
Oxford
OX1 3AZ
☎ 01865 277280
The collection of scientific instruments from antiquity to the twentieth century is housed in the oldest museum building in the UK, which was opened in 1683. Astrolabes, watches, clocks, and of particular interest, is Boyle's seventeenth-century pressure chamber, which he used in experiments to formulate his law that governs air and space travel. Also there is the original penicillin apparatus and Einstein's blackboard.

BOOKSHOPS

Blackwell's
53 Broad Street
Oxford
OX1 3BQ
☎ 01865 792792
A cornucopia of books can be found in the street besides the main store, where you also find one of the best cafés in town. Music books at no's 23–25, children's at no. 8 and the Art and Poster Shop at no. 27.

Borders (Books, Music, Video and Café)
9 Magdalen Street
Oxford
☎ 01865 203901
The second largest book chain in the world offers booklovers late night shopping until 11pm except Sunday. The music section that allows digital listening to any CD in the store and the café where you drink coffee as well as beer are definite attractions. It also has the largest magazine selection outside London and an astonishing range of newspapers in different languages. Browsers are welcome.

Unsworth
15 Turl Street
Oxford
OX1 3DQ
☎ 01865 727 928 Fax: 01865 727 206
Website: www.unsworth.com
A place to find bargains in new books in classics, history, arts, literature and social sciences.

The Classics Bookshop
3 Turl Street
Oxford
OX1 3DQ
☎ 01865 726466 Fax: 01865 241421
E-mail:
classicsbookshop@hotmail.com
A good source for second-hand books on classical antiquity as the range includes Greek and Latin texts, literature, classics, archaeology, ancient history, philosophy and philology. Also has antiquarian books and prints of Oxford.

Oxford Unviversity Press (OUP)
116–117 High Street
Oxford
☎ 01865 242913
A bookshop which is a showcase for OUP, the largest university publisher in the world. The first book was printed in 1478 and in spite of traditional ties that require a group of delegates from the university to approve each book prior to publication, OUP produces profits of some £30 million a year for the university. The most popular book in the shop is still the Oxford English Dictionary.

Waterstones
Broad Street
Oxford
☎ 01865 790212
For visitors who like to indulge in serendipity, they may wish to browse in second-hand bookshops, such as **Waterfields** at 52 High Street, the bookshop in the covered market and **Arcadia** at 4 St Michael's Street.

CLIMATE

Oxford has a damp climate with frequent mist as it is situated in the Thames Valley. Expect rain at any time. For weather information check ☎ 0891 505 306

CONFERENCE CENTRE

Oxford is an important conference centre and has an availability of over 6,000 beds. The university with its 36 conference-active colleges is the provider of facilities. Groups can experience the tradition of Oxford, including dining in a candlelit banquet in a college hall, listening to Evensong in a chapel, playing croquet on the lawn or savouring champagne and strawberries while punting down the River Cherwell.

Conference Oxford
118 High Street
Oxford
OX1 4BX
☎ 01865 276190
Email: conference.oxford@univ.ox.ac.uk

Williams F1 Conference Centre
Grove,
Wantage,
Oxfordshire,
England OX12 ODQ
☎ +44(0)1235 777822 or
777148
Fax:+44(0)1235 777730
E-mail:
jayne.dillon@williamsf1.com
Conference Centre Manager
Direct: ☎ +44(0)1235 777147

Houses the Williams F1 Conference Centre and Grand Prix
Collection. Over 31,000
square feet given over to 41
genuine running race cars
providing an interactive tour
through 25 years of Wiliams
successes on the track, with

the remainder of the space given
over to conference and entertaining facilities.
The Williams collection is not
open to the general public but
group tours can be arranged by
appointment.

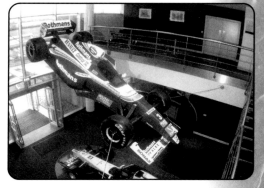

CULTURAL EVENTS

February
Torpids
College rowing races held in the
sixth week of the Hilary term.

May
May Day
On 1 May at 6am Magdalen
College choir sings from
Magdalen Tower accompanied
by Morris dancing in Radcliffe
Square and Broad Street.
Lord Mayor's Parade
On the Spring Bank Holiday
decorated floats start at St Giles
along a route to South Parks.
Eights Week
Intercollegiate rowing races
when each crew attempts to
'bump' or touch the boat in
front.
Beating the bounds
On Ascension Day starts at St
Michael's Church, Northgate.
Art Week

Workshops of local artists and
crafts people open their work-
shops to the public.
June
Encaenia (Dedication Festival)
The ceremony occurs at noon on
the first Wednesday in the week
following Trinity Term.
August
Oxford Regatta
Organised by City of Oxford
Rowing Club (☎ 01865 242576).

September
St Giles' Fair
Held on the first Monday and
Tuesday.

December
Chapel choirs perform at Christ
Church, Magdalen and New
College. Apply for tickets to
performances by mid November.

DISABLED ACCESS

Oxford Shopmobility, Level 1a of Westgate Shopping Centre Multi Storey car park. Opening hours Monday to Friday 09.30 - 16.00 Contact Shopmobility Co-ordinator: Oxford Shopmobility Scheme, C/o Built Environment, Ramsay House, 10 St Ebbes Street, Oxford OX1 1PT
More information on City Council's web site
A scheme funded by the City Council for borrowing a self-propelled or battery operated wheelchair or scooter to shop in the City Centre. Booking is required but there is no charge. ☎ 01865 248737

DRIVING

In the UK, driving is on the left hand side of the road and seat belts must be worn at all times.

GARDENS

Under the National Gardens Scheme residents open their gardens to the public from March to October. A booklet is available in bookshops, which provides a list in Oxfordshire, including College gardens. (Check *Oxford Mail* and *Oxford Times* for openings).
Gardens can also be found in parks:
South Park at the bottom of Headington Hill;
Cutterslowe Park, off the ring road in north Oxford;
Bury Knowle Park in Headington;
Florence Park in Cowley;
Christ Church Meadow at St Aldates;
University Parks at Parks Road;
Shotover Country Park at Old Road;
Port Meadow at Walton Well Street.

LANGUAGE SCHOOLS

Anglo World
108 Banbury Road
Oxford
OX2 6JU
☎ 01865 515 808

Eckersley
14 Friars Entry
Oxford
OX1 8BZ
☎ 01865 721 268

King's
St Joseph's Hall
Temple Road
Oxford
OX2 2UJ
☎ 01865 711 829

**Oxford Brookes
Language Services**
Gipsy Lane Campus
Oxford
OX3 0BP
☎ 01865 483 692

OLT
9 Blue Boar Street
Oxford
OX1 4EZ
☎ 01865 793 088

Lake School of English
16 Park End Street
Oxford
OX1 1JQ
☎ 01865 724 312

MEDIA

The *Oxford Mail* and *The Oxford Times* (at weekends) are the two newspapers in the city which cover local events.

MUSIC: CONCERTS AND OPERA

Sheldonian Theatre
Venue for numerous musical events, including performances by various orchestras.

The City of Oxford Orchestra
☎ 01865 744457

Music at Oxford
☎ 01865 798600

The Oxford Philomusica
See website
www.oxfordphil.com

Jacqueline due Pre Music Building
St Hilda's College
☎ 01865 276821

Holywell Music Room
In addition to regular concerts, coffee concerts are held on Sundays at 11am.
☎ 01865 798600

College Choirs

Choral evensong is an essential part of the Anglican service and Christ Church and Magdalen established special schools for choristers. Sunday evensong in college chapels is open to the public.

Opera

There is no opera house in Oxford, but performances are held at:

Apollo Playhouse
George Street
☎ 01865 244544

Garsington Manor
Garsington
Nr Oxford
☎ 01865 361636

PUBLIC TRANSPORT

There is an excellent system provided by buses. See Park & Ride page 90, Travel Information.

RESTAURANTS

Introduction to the Restaurants of Oxford

I first became involved in the restaurant scene in Oxford some 25 years ago and I have been surprised by how much it has expanded since then.

Oxford now has the most varied and cosmopolitan range of restaurants, outside London appealing to the young, the sophisticated and the traditionalist. Whether you are looking for a quick bite or a relaxing meal with all of the trimmings and a pleasant ambience, there should be a restaurant, café or bar to suit you and your pocket. Standards may vary but this guide should help you to decide on the best available. Enjoy yourself.

By Jeremy Mogford

Fact File

Quod Bar and Grill
92–94 High Street
☎ 01865 202505
Open every day.
A contemporary interior with huge dramatic paintings around the walls, part of the boutique hotel the Old Bank. Italian style cooking with chargrilled meats and fish, pasta, salads and risottos. A place to see Oxford society, where town meets gown.

Restaurant Elizabeth
82 St Aldates
Oxford
☎ 01865 242230
Closed on Mondays
Two dining rooms, one with oak panelling and the other with a decorated plasterwork ceiling in a seventeenth-century building which overlooks Christ Church gardens. The cuisine is French with Spanish and Greek additions. It has a small à la carte menu and a fixed price menu at lunch time. Situated on the first floor, entry can only be gained by ringing the doorbell. Owner Antonio Lopez, presides to give a warm welcome.

Gee's
61 Banbury Road
Oxford
☎ 01865 553540
Open daily
The setting of one of the most fashionable restaurants in Oxford is unusual, it's a Victorian conservatory. Air conditioning, an attentive staff, a good à la carte menu, particularly the seafood dishes and a diverse wine list. Express lunch is a bargain.

Le Petit Blanc
71–72 Walton Street
Oxford
☎ 01865 510999
Open daily; Sunday dinner only
An introduction to the French chef, Raymond Blanc's traditional dishes which are served in a contemporary setting. Fixed price menu also available. If you like the food in the brasserie, you can gourmandize by visiting Blanc's fourteenth-century manor house about 10 miles out of Oxford, **Le Manoir Aux Quat' Saisons** in Great Milton. ☎ 01844 278881.

Cherwell Boathouse
Bardwell Road
Oxford
☎ 01865 552746
Open daily, April–October
Situated in a beautiful setting along the banks of the river and punts are available from March to September. Ideal spot for warm weather. Interesting wine list.

Browns
5–11 Woodstock Road
Oxford
☎ 01865 511995
Open daily, 11am–11.30pm.
A large well-established restaurant where families are welcome and which offers breakfasts as well as lunch and dinner.

Pizza Express
The Golden Cross
Cornmarket Street
Oxford
☎ 01865 790442
Open daily
An unusual place to eat pizzas as it is located in a historic courtyard which has links with Shakespeare and the Martyrs. There is a sixteenth-century wall painting inside and in summer you can eat alfresco.

Convocation Coffee House
University Church of St Mary
(entrance opposite Radcliffe
Camera)
☎ 01865 794334
The former fourteenth-century
meeting place for the university's governing body now serves
lunches and teas with pastries
and cakes.

The Parsonage
Restaurant and Bar
1 Banbury Road
Oxford
☎ 01865 310210
Open daily
A quiet haven with a club atmosphere, it serves breakfasts,
lunch and dinner until 11pm.
Attached to the Old Parsonage
hotel, it is a discrete rendezvous.

The Trout Inn
195 Godstow Road
Wolvercote
☎ 01865 302071
A pub popular with visitors
because of its beautiful situation
at the Medley weir of the
Thames, its strolling peacocks
and historic interior, with fireplaces. There is a ruin of an
abbey opposite where the Fair
Rosamund, King Henry II's
mistress, was buried.

Ice Cream

George and Davis
55 Little Clarendon Street
Oxford
☎ 01865 516652
Branch: 94 Pembroke Street
☎ 01865 245952
Open daily, 8am–midnight.
Oxford's own home-made ice-
cream with natural ingredients.

Coffee Shops

There are many coffee shops in
the city, including brands like
Starbucks, Coffee Republic and
local varieties like The Grand
Cafe and The Rose in the High

For the best sandwhiches try Pret
a Manger in the Cornmarket.

SHOPPING

Oxford provides a unique shopping experience. Unlike most cities
we still retain an astonishing number of independent retailers,
ranging from booksellers to specialists in antique glass and silver,
maps and prints, handmade shoes, jewellery and timeless fashion -
all backed up by knowledgeable and helpful service. Certainly the
18th century Covered Market is an experience not to be missed.
And alongside famous streets like the High, the Broad and the Turl,
Oxford also boasts an impressive spectrum of multiple retailers
with stores like Debenhams, Next, Gap and M&S in the pedestrianised centre. Don't miss us!

By Julian Blackwell

Pens Plus

70 High Street
OX1 4BD
☎ 01865 241174

In a city of books and scholars, it is apt to find a shop that is dedicated to writing equipment from quills, to calligraphy, limited editions and space pens. They also repair vintage and modern pens.

Neals Yard Remedies

56 High Street
OX1 4AS
☎ 01865 245436

The well-known herbal shop with its wide selection of natural remedies many of which were grown in the Botanic Garden opposite. Expect to find everything from herbal teas to cosmetics, toiletries, essential oils and bach flower remedies.

Reginald Davies

34 High Street
OX1 4AN
☎ 01865 200915

Antique silver from seventeenth century, including items from colleges, old Sheffield plate and antique jewellery.

Frederick Tranter

37 High Street
OX1 4AN
☎ 01865 243543

A tobacco blender and cigar merchant dating back to the nineteenth century has a full range of Cuban cigars, snuffs, pipes and blended tobacco including Virginia, aromatics, American style, straight Virginias, navy cuts and flakes, mixtures and fine cuts. Pipes, particularly the long reading briars are popular with fellows and the snuffs, including aniseed, strawberry and mint flavours are favoured by undergraduates.

Laurie Lee

36 High Street
OX1 4AN
☎ 01865 244197

An unusual combination of eighteenth to nineteenth-century antique tables, glass and old keyboard musical instruments. Glassware can be safely shipped worldwide.

Magna Gallery

41 High Street
OX1 4AP
☎ 01865 245805

A fine selection of English county maps from 1579 to 1850, coloured or black and white prints.

A view of Cornmarket Street which is pedestrianised

BY APPOINTMENT TO
H.M. QUEEN ELIZABETH II
ROBE MAKERS

BY APPOINTMENT TO
H.R.H. THE DUKE OF EDINBURGH
ROBE MAKERS

BY APPOINTMENT TO
H.M. QUEEN ELIZABETH
THE QUEEN MOTHER
ROBE MAKERS

BY APPOINTMENT TO
H.R.H. THE PRINCE OF WALES
ROBE MAKERS

ROBE MAKERS & TAILORS SINCE THE YEAR 1689

Ede and Ravenscroft evokes the authentic British look for every occasion, supplying fine quality clothes to men who appreciate timeless style.

Ready to wear, made to order and bespoke tailoring. Country and formal wear, morning and evening dress. Fine cotton shirts, exclusive silk ties, footwear and gentlemen's accessories.

119 High Street Oxford Tel: 01865 242756
Monday to Saturday 9 am - 5.30 pm

London 93 Chancery Lane London WC2 Tel: 020 7405 3906
8 Burlington Gardens Savile Row London W1 Tel: 020 7734 5450
2 Gracechurch Street London EC3 Tel: 020 7929 1848
Cambridge 71-72 Trumpington Street Cambridge Tel: 01223 350048
Edinburgh 46 Frederick Street Edinburgh Tel: 0131 225 6354
www.edeandravenscroft.co.uk

Antiques on High
85 High Street
OX1 4BG
☎ 01865 251075
An antique emporium with an interesting selection from 35 dealers offering a wide range of collectables, including antiquities, jewellery and books.

Sanders
104 High Street
OX1 4BW
☎ 01865 242590
Situated in a sixteenth-century building, the rare print and map shop complements your visit as you can invariably buy a print of most of the buildings in the city, including colleges. The selection of prints covers portraits, caricatures, Japanese, sporting, natural history, decorative, topographical and military/maritime. A rare Gilroy coloured cartoon from Punch was on display with a tag of £3,700.

Hobbs
115 High Street
OX1 4BX
☎ 01865 249437
A branch of the top British designer, Marilyn Anselm, who developed the concept of capsule wardrobes, which integrates clothes, shoes and accessories.

Payne and Son
131 High Street
OX1 4DH
☎ 01865 243787
A late nineteenth-century shop with a good selection of antique and modern silver, which is run by the family. A speciality is reproduction college silver, including a range of drinking and tumbling cups from liqueur size to ale size, which make an interesting present.

University of Oxford Shop
106 High Street
OX1 4BW
☎ 01865 724 379
A souvenir shop with a variety of items such as ties, cufflinks, t-shirts and porcelainware.

Covered Market
Three entrances into the market between the Mitre Inn and Natwest Bank in the High. There are several speciality shops, including cheese, knitwear, organic butchers, delicatessen, homemade biscuits and a tea and coffee merchant.

Edinburgh Woollen Mill
141 High Street
OX1 4DS
☎ 01865 242113
A good selection of knitwear, including tartans, bargains.

Gill and Company
128A High Street
OX1
☎ 01865 242058
An ironmonger which has been in existence since the sixteenth century.

Speciality Shops

Ede and Ravenscroft
119 High Street
Oxford
OX1 4BX
☎ 01865 242756
Men's bespoke and ready to wear clothes shop which has eye-catching windows. A recent display featured the bespoke book for 19 September 1967 when Professor Tolkien ordered a black velvet smoking jacket. Academic gowns and ceremonial robes for which they have four Royal warrants are a speciality. Their tweeds are popular with Americans and many locals order bespoke cloaks.

Castell & Sons
13 Broad Street
OX1 3AS
☎ 01865 244 000
A varsity shop with a range of souvenirs.

Shepherd and Woodward
109-113 High Street
Oxford
OX1 4BT
☎ 01865 249491
A menswear shop that also specialises in Oxford University College clothing and academic

gowns for hire and purchase. One of the directors, Dennis Venables, has produced an excellent booklet on academic dress of the University of Oxford that enables readers to peek behind the traditions of wearing gowns and gain an insight into the arcane ceremonies for which they are required.

THEATRES

Apollo
George Street
☎ 01865 244544

Burton-Taylor
Gloucester Street
☎ 01865 798600

Oxford Playhouse
Beaumont Street
☎ 01865 798600

TIPPING

Most restaurants expect 10–15 per cent service charge and add this to your bill. This amount is normal when dealing with services such as taxis. The only exception is in pubs.

TOILETS WITH FACILITIES

Toilets with facilities for people with disabilities (with National Key Entry Scheme) at:
Market St, daytime
Speedwell St, March- October
Oxpens Coach Park ,24hrs;
Gloucester Green, 24 hrs
St Clement's car park 24 hrs
Oxford Railway Station
National Key Entry Scheme: keys available from Oxford Railway Station, Tourist Information Centre and St. Algate's Chambers
☎ 01865 726871/252067

TOURIST INFORMATION CENTRE

15-16 Broad Street
Oxford
OX1 3AS
☎ 01865 726871 Fax: 01865 240261
Email: tic@oxford.gov.uk
Open: Monday–Saturday, 9.30am–5pm. Sunday 10am–3.30pm.

TRAVEL INFORMATION

Oxford is well served by air, road and rail connection.

Air

Heathrow airport
45 miles (72km) from the city and there are regular coach services to and from the airport.

Gatwick airport
85 miles (136km) from the city and services run regularly.

Birmingham airport
65 miles (104km) from the city and there are both train and coach services.

Train

Regular train services from Paddington Station, London to Oxford.

Bus

Two companies operate services between London and Oxford, the Oxford Tube and City Link, and there is also a national network through National Express.

Car

The city is well served by motorways, the M25 from Heathrow and the M40 from London.

Park & Ride Scheme

Frequent buses link these car parks to the Oxford City Centre. 'Easy Access' buses for Wheelchair users. Pay & Display system for car parking at Peartree, Redbridge & Seacourt car parks of 50p per day. Parking at Thornhill car park is free.
Car Parks are located at Redbridge, Pear Tree, Seacourt, Thornhill
Fares: Adult Single £1.20, Day Return £1.60. Children under 3 travel free when accompanied by an adult.

Parking for the Disabled

Park and Ride – places available adjacent to bus stops
Westgate – places available on level 4 adjacent to the shopping level.
On-Street Parking – special bays marked.
Disabled persons showing both parts of the Orange Badge may park for free in any of the on-street parking spaces.
Standard charges apply in off-street car parks.

BORDERS®
BOOKS / MUSIC / VIDEO & CAFE
9 Magdalen Street, Oxford OX1 3AD
01865 203901

- **B**rowse our selection of over 120,000 book titles, 25,000 CDs and 5,000 videos/DVDs as well as an extensive range of newspapers and magazines.

- **O**rdering and worldwide delivery of any books, CDs and films available on the international market that may not be in stock.

- **R**elax on comfy armchairs or sofas, in a warm friendly environment whilst reading or listening to music.

- **D**iscover our events calendar packed with entertainment including readings, book signings, children's events and live music.

- **E**njoy convenient hours to suit your lifestyle, 9.00 am - 11.00 pm Monday to Saturday and 11.00 am - 5.00 pm Sunday.

- **R**evolutionary Digital listening system so you can sample all 25,000 CDs in stock before you buy.

- **S**avour our range of coffees, sodas, alcoholic drinks, light meals and snacks in our spacious café.

Business and academic accounts (including competitive discounts) are also available. Contact Borders for further details.

Index

LANDMARK VISITORS

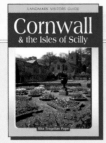

Cornwall*
ISBN: 1 84306 034 5
256pp, £10.95

Devon
ISBN: 1 84306 003 5
224pp, £10.95

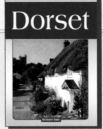

Dorset
ISBN: 1 84306 001 9
240pp, £10.95

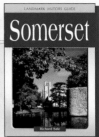

Somerset
ISBN: 1 901522 40 7
224pp, £9.95

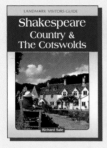

Shakespeare Country & The Cotswolds
ISBN: 1 84306 002 7
208pp, £10.95

Lake District*
ISBN: 1 901522 38 5
224pp, £9.95

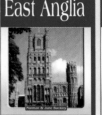

East Anglia
ISBN: 1 901522 58 X
224pp, £9.95

Scotland*
ISBN: 1 901522 18 0
288pp, £11.95

Jersey
ISBN: 1 901522 93 8
224pp, £10.95

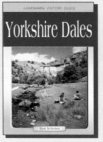

Yorkshire Dales*
ISBN: 1 901522 41 5
208pp, £10.95

Harrogate
ISBN: 1 901522 55 5
96pp, £2.99

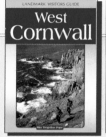

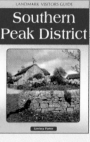
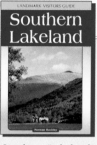
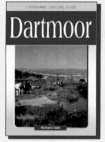

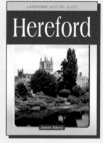

Published by:
Landmark Publishing Ltd,
Ashbourne Hall, Cokayne Avenue, Ashbourne, Derbyshire DE6 1EJ England
E-mail landmark@clara.net Web-site www.landmarkpublishing.co.uk

ISBN 1 84306 022 1

© **Farrol Kahn 2002**

1st Landmark edition 2002

British Library Cataloguing in Publication Data:
A catalogue record for this book is available from the British Library

Print: Gutenberg Press Ltd, Malta
Cartography: Mark Titterton
Design: Mark Titterton

Front cover: Annual academic procession, Radcliffe square
Back Cover top: University Museum
Back Cover bottom: The High

Photograph credits: Anita Zabilevska — back cover top; 31t; 31b; 34; 35b;
42t; 42m; 46tl; 46b; 88. Williams F1; 81. All other photography by Mark
Titterton including front cover and back cover bottom.